Fourth edition

SUCCESS AT THE ENQUIRY DESK

Successful enquiry answering – every time

Tim Buckley Owen

facet publishing

© Tim Buckley Owen 1996, 1997, 1998, 2000, 2003

Published by
Facet Publishing
7 Ridgmount Street
London WC1E 7AE

Facet Publishing (formerly Library Association Publishing) is wholly owned by CILIP: the Chartered Institute of Library and Information Professionals.

First published in the *Successful LIS Professional* series,
    edited by Sheila Pantry 1996
First revised edition 1997
Second revised edition 1998
Third edition 2000
This fourth edition 2003

British Library Cataloguing in Publication Data
A catalogue record for this book is available from the British Library.

ISBN 1-85604-477-7

The Successful LIS Professional series, edited by Sheila Pantry OBE

Liz MacLachlan   Making project management work for you
Ailsa Masterton   Getting results with time management
Sheila Pantry   Dealing with aggression and violence in your workplace
Sheila Pantry and Peter Griffiths   Becoming a successful intrapreneur
Sheila Pantry and Peter Griffiths   Developing a successful service plan
Sheila Pantry and Peter Griffiths   Your successful LIS career
Elizabeth Parker   Managing your organization's records

Typeset in 11/14 pt Aldine 721 by Facet Publishing.
Printed and made in Great Britain by MPG Books Ltd, Bodmin, Cornwall.

Contents

Introduction   v

Five fundamentals for successful enquiry answering   viii

Nine steps to successful enquiry answering: the *Success at the enquiry desk* enquiry form   ix

Twenty-five multi-purpose reference sources you can't afford to ignore   xii

1   What do you really want?   1
    How to make sure you really understand the question
                Avoiding misunderstandings   2
                Asking the right questions   5
                Agreeing the task   8
                Finding out how long you've got   17

2   Not too much, now   19
    Too much information is as bad as too little
                Information overload   20
                How much does your enquirer need?   21
                Working out the level of specialism   24
                Earmarking and eliminating potential sources   24

3   Help! My mind's gone blank   26
    Techniques for getting started
                What will the final answer look like?   26
                What kinds of sources will do the job?   28
                Identifying actual sources   30

4   More on choosing sources   34
    How to decide which is the best medium for the job
                Focus, dynamism, complexity   35
                Print, portable databases, online   38
                The right medium for the job?   39

5   Do I really know what I'm looking for?   44
    Tips for efficient search strategies
                Where to search first   44

Searching systematically   46
Getting the best out of the web   53
Rapid reading   59

6   Quick! Time's running out   61
How to meet deadlines every time
Vital versus urgent   62
Your working timetable   64
A compromise answer?   67
Progress reports   69

7   Can't find the answer – what now?   70
What to do if your chosen sources fail
Preparing your enquirer for disappointment   71
Looking for outside help   72
Asking authors or editors   74
Buying the information in   75
Settling for an alternative answer   76

8   Success! Now let's add some value   78
Presenting your answer well is part of the job
Have you really answered it?   78
What to leave out   79
Presenting what's left   80

9   Sign-off: what can we learn from this enquiry?   85
Using completed enquiries to develop your services
How successful were you?   86
How long did it take to answer?   87
Did you have to refer the enquiry elsewhere?   88
Did you discover any useful new sources?   90
Looking to the future   91
Your goal: successful enquiry answering – every time   93

10   Guide to key reference sources   94
Full details of key sources mentioned in the book, with annotations

Index   111

Introduction

Every time I've come to revise this book I've started by saying 'There's never been a better time to be in the library and information profession,' and each time it's been more true than before. It's still true; but now, as internet use becomes more and more widespread, the stakes have been raised. Everyone's an expert searcher these days – or so they think – and the pressure on us as information professionals to perform even more effectively becomes ever more acute.

Should we fear this? Certainly not! For years people in this profession bemoaned the fact that decision-makers didn't recognize the value of information or appreciate the special knowledge and skills that we as library and information professionals could bring to bear in managing and exploiting it. Well, now they do recognize the value of information, and it's up to us to ensure that they also understand that we can add to that value even more.

There's a saying amongst theatrical folk: amateurs rehearse to make sure everything goes right; professionals rehearse to make sure nothing goes wrong. It's spot on as far as enquiry work is concerned; lots of things can go wrong, and it's up to us to know where the pitfalls lie, to anticipate problems and avoid them. DIY searching tools are available to everyone now; our job as professionals is, firstly, to use those tools more effectively, and then to bring in more efficient specialist tools when the DIY ones show that they're not up to the job. How do we find out what those tools are? How do we use them effectively? That's what this book is all about.

It's an introduction to techniques that can help you deal with enquiries on any subject, whether or not there are any publications about it. These techniques make use of the web where appropriate, but they meld it with other sources, both printed and electronic. The examples used throughout the book largely reflect my own experience in social science, current affairs and business information. But the techniques work just as effectively for enquiries about technology, medicine, arts or law. Certainly we need to have some key information sources always at our fingertips, but that's not fundamentally what enquiry answering is about.

In essence, successful enquiry answering is about applied common sense, exercise of the imagination and shared experience. As more and more emphasis is laid on information handling skills in formal education, and growing numbers of people engage in self-directed lifelong learning using the internet, then techniques such as these will become more widespread across the population as a whole. What we professionals need to do is systematize these techniques, learn from our experience, and keep our skills in the peak of condition at all times. We need to attend training courses and briefing sessions. We need to gain qualifications – such as those currently offered by CILIP: the Chartered Institute of Library and Information Professionals and the much wider range of qualifications soon to come – that will provide evidence of our competence to our enquirers and to potential employers. In short, we need to demonstrate the commitment that people expect of professionals.

One thing the internet has done is to increase dramatically the range of opportunities for professional enquiry answering activity. This is no longer the exclusive preserve of the person sitting in a book-lined room – although, as this book will demonstrate, print on paper remains a remarkably effective medium for storing and retrieving information, whatever the internet pundits may say. Nevertheless, the extraordinary technological developments of the last decade or so have meant that we are just as likely to be working in a call centre – using only a few printed sources and largely reliant on electronic information media – or we might even be constantly on the move, with only a laptop and a mobile phone as our means of access to the world of knowledge that we need to do our job.

Nor should we assume any more that we have to rely exclusively on material that's in the public domain – printed publications, online databases, other public enquiry services. We're just as likely to be exploiting unpublished sources as well: internal documents and datasets, even the knowledge in people's heads. Increasingly, this job is not simply about providing support to decision-makers but about adding value in our own right – not merely about seeking out the best sources for the job, but about exploiting them and turning them into new information sources, fit for the purpose. It's about going the extra mile; years ago we may simply have been lookers-up, but now, increasingly, we need to be publishers as well.

It really is true; there has never been a better time to be in the information profession. So you need to start somewhere, and I hope this book will help you grasp the basic principles of one of the world's most fascinating professions. After that, the opportunities are limited only by your own imagination.

Tim Buckley Owen

Five fundamentals for successful enquiry answering

It's all too easy for your mind to go completely blank when faced with the challenge of a new enquiry. If you can remember nothing else, try to keep these five fundamentals in mind. They'll help you get started, and keep you on track.

1 Never take an enquiry at face value, always ask a question back – because you never know where it may lead.
2 Start by imagining what the final answer will look like – that will help you focus on the best sources for the job.
3 Jot down the search terms you're going to use in a structured hierarchy, not just a random list – that will help you search more efficiently and quickly.
4 If you can't find the answer, ask yourself who really needs to know this information – that should give you ideas for who to ask for help.
5 Make sure you always add value when presenting your answer – that will demonstrate your professionalism.

Nine steps to successful enquiry answering: the *Success at the enquiry desk* enquiry form

Enquiry forms come in all shapes and sizes. At their most basic, they may simply have somewhere to record the question and the enquirer's contact details, followed by a large blank space for you to use as you wish. More complex forms may require you to record your search strategy, or even include suggestions for sources you could try. A growing number of library and information services are developing electronic enquiry recording; networked, this can enable any member of staff to keep track of progress on enquiries and can facilitate collaborative enquiry answering; it can also provide an audit trail for charging purposes. On the other hand, some libraries and information units don't use forms at all, but rely on notebooks or even scrap paper.

Our enquiry form (on the next two pages) tries to give you as much help as possible. In nine steps, it takes you through the entire process, from recording the question to the final sign-off, when the enquiry has been answered successfully and you are considering what follow-up action the enquiry may require – recording a useful new reference source in your information file, for example, or a new website that you could bookmark as a favourite for future use. We make sure that you analyse the enquiry accurately (step 3), and that you plan your search strategy properly (step 5). At steps 4 and 6, we make suggestions on possible sources you could try – first the types of source that might be suitable, and then some actual titles. In fact, our enquiry form follows the structure of this book.

We've had to compress it to fit it onto the book's small pages (you'd certainly need a lot more space for sections 6 and 7 than we allow here), and what you see as a pair of facing pages would actually be the front and back of a paper form. If it were electronic, then the lists that you see on the second page would work very well as checkable pull-down menus. If you find it helpful as a model, then you may like to adapt it – in printed or electronic form – for use in your own library or information unit.

1 QUESTION (as much detail as possible)	2 ENQUIRER DETAILS
	Name:
	Organization:
	Address:
	Postcode:
	Tel:
	Fax:
Enquiry taken by:	E-mail:
Deadline:	Special contact instructions:

3 ENQUIRY ANALYSIS	4 ENQUIRY TYPE
Who?	**Focus**
What?	Broad: ❏ Narrow: ❏
When?	**Dyanamism**
Where?	Static: ❏ Dynamic: ❏
Why?	**Complexity**
How?	Single issue: ❏ Multi-faceted: ❏
	Viability
What will the final answer look like?	Can't be answered in-house: ❏
	Not available in a published source: ❏
	(See over for possible types of source to use)

5 SEARCH STRATEGY
Broader terms:

ROOT TERMS

Narrower terms:

Related terms:

6 POSSIBLE STARTER SOURCES (See over for suggestions)	7 SEARCH RESULTS

8 ANSWER	9 SIGN-OFF
	Enquiry completed by:
	Answer delivered by:
	Success...
	Complete: ❏ Partial: ❏ Compromise: ❏
	Enquiry referred to:
	Time taken to answer: ....hrs ....mins
	When completed:
	Delivered on time? Yes: ❏ No: ❏
	Reasons if late:
	Follow-up action (eg add new information or source to information file):

TYPES OF SOURCE TO CONSIDER
(Section 4)

Broad
Entry in a general encyclopaedia
Chapter in a textbook
Complete textbook

Narrow
Entry in a special encyclopaedia
Index entry in a textbook
Special report
Journal article
Table in a statistical journal
Entry in a directory
Database record
Web page

Static
Encyclopaedia or dictionary
Textbook
Selection of journal articles
Statistical time series
Directory
CD-ROM database

Dynamic
Current newspaper
Recent journal
Latest statistical journal
Press release
Online news service – proprietary or web
Audiotex

Single issue
Printed source if easy to find
Database/web if hard to find

Multi-faceted
Online database/web
CD-ROM database

Can't be answered in-house
Library or information unit guide
Nearby public or educational library
Personal contact

Not available in a published source
Specialist organization
Author of nearly relevant publication
Editor of relevant periodical
Personal contact

POSSIBLE STARTER SOURCES
(Section 6)

Identifying basic reference sources
Know It All, Find It Fast
Walford's Guide to Reference Material
Current British Directories

Finding contacts for further information
Directory of British Associations
Councils, Committees & Boards
Aslib Directory of Information Sources
Hollis UK Press & Public Relations Annual
World of Learning

Tracing news items
BBC News Online

Tracing articles
British Humanities Index
Applied Social Sciences Index
Abstracts in New Technologies and Engineering

Tracing books
British National Bibliography
Whitaker LibWeb

Identifying websites
The Public Librarian's Guide to the Internet

Identifying journals and newspapers
Willing's Press Guide
Benn's Media

Identifying statistical sources
National Statistics website
Sources of Non-official UK Statistics

Comprehensive facts & figures
Whitaker's Almanac
UK... the Official Yearbook of the United
   Kingdom

Events & dates
Keesing's Record of World Events
Annual Register

Statistics
Annual Abstract of Statistics
Social Trends

Twenty-five multi-purpose reference sources you can't afford to ignore

Ever since you were a child at school, you've been looking things up – using encyclopaedias, dictionaries, phone books, recipe books, Who's Whos. By now you'll also be familiar with your own in-house catalogues and finding aids, including any internal information files that your colleagues may have compiled. You'll know about your collection of CD-ROMs of reference works, newspapers, periodicals or statistics, and you should have access to the world wide web. In other words, you already know a great deal about how to find information.

But for really successful enquiry work, there's a small core of more specialist reference sources that it's worth knowing about. On the next page you'll find a quick checklist of some of the most useful ones, and there's a full guide to these and other sources, with annotations, in Chapter 10 of this book.

Most of these sources started as printed publications, but many are now also available electronically – via the web or on CD-ROM – and some are web-only. Where possible, I have indicated in the guide to key reference sources when a source is also available in electronic form; *Know it all, find it fast* (no. 1 in this list) will often give you this information as well. Access to official websites (government or international organizations) should be free, but on many other sites the information will be password-protected and available only on subscription at commercial prices. In some cases, though, you can buy information by credit card on a pay-per-view basis.

It's difficult to carry too many sources of this kind in your head – 25 seems a good number to start with. So try to become familiar with them (and their international equivalents); they'll get you started on a great many of the enquiries you'll have to deal with.

Purpose	Item number	Title	International equivalents
Identifying basic reference sources	1 2 3	Know It All, Find It Fast Walford's Guide to Reference Material Current British Directories	[Know It All, Find It Fast] Ulrich's Periodicals Directory
Finding contacts for further information	4	Directory of British Associations	Encyclopaedia of Associations: International Organizations Europa Directory of International Organizations World Directory of Trade and Business Associations Yearbook of International Organizations
	5 6 7 8	Councils, Committees & Boards Aslib Directory of Information Sources in the United Kingdom Hollis UK Press & Public Relations Annual World of Learning	 Hollis Europe: the Directory of European Public Relations & PR Networks [World of Learning]
Tracing news items	9	BBC News Online	[BBC News Online] Keesing's Record of World Events
Tracing articles	10 11 12	British Humanities Index Applied Social Sciences Index and Abstracts Abstracts in New Technologies and Engineering	Humanities Index/Abstracts/full text Sociological Abstracts Social Aciences Index/Abstracts/full text Applied Science Index & Abstracts/full text General Science Abstracts/full text British Library – inside web Emerald Ingenta Wilson OmniFile Full Text Mega Edition
Tracing books	13 14	British National Bibliography Whitaker LibWeb	British Library Public Catalogue [Whitaker LibWeb] Global Books in Print
Identifying websites	15	The Public Librarian's Guide to the Internet	[The Public Librarian's Guide to the Internet]
Identifying journals & newspapers	16 17	Willing's Press Guide Benn's Media	[Willing's] [Benn's] Ulrich's Periodicals Directory
Identifying statistical sources	18 19	National Statistics website Sources of Non-official UK Statistics	United Nations Statistics Division website World Directory of Non-official Statistical Sources
Comprehensive facts & figures	20 21	Whitaker's Almanac UK... the Official Yearbook of the United Kingdom of Great Britain and Northern Ireland	 Europa World Yearbook Statesman's Yearbook
Events & dates	22 23	Keesing's Record of World Events Annual Register	[Keesing's Record of World Events] [Annual Register]
Statistics	24 25	Annual Abstract of Statistics Social Trends	United Nations Statistical Yearbook Eurostat Yearbook World Marketing Data & Statistics

Chapter 1
What do you really want?
How to make sure you really understand the question

In this chapter you'll find out how to:

➤ **avoid misunderstandings**
➤ **ask the right questions**
➤ **agree the task**
➤ **find out how long you've got to do it.**

There's a story told of a London taxi driver some years ago who picked up an American fare outside Victoria Station. There was a big Egyptology exhibition on at the British Museum at the time. 'Take me to Tutankhamun,' the lady drawled. So the cabbie did. Thirty minutes later he dropped her at a rather down-at-heel patch of open space in the south-west London suburbs, called 'Tooting Common'.

It's an apocryphal tale, no doubt. But it does show the problems you can hit when dealing with what seems like the simplest of enquiries. Some of your queries will come orally, face-to-face. The possibilities for misunderstandings are endless – accent, articulation, assumptions, all can send you scurrying off in totally the wrong direction, wasting both your time and the enquirer's. But with face-to-face enquiries, you are at least offered lots of clues; most of what we communicate is non-verbal, so you can glean what you can from facial expression, eye contact, body language. You are deprived of these clues when your queries come in by phone, and you have even less to go on when they arrive in written form – by e-mail, fax or post. So the first task has to be: no matter how your enquiry comes in, always make sure you understand the question.

Avoiding misunderstandings

Remember when you were doing your exams, and teachers and lecturers dinned into you the lesson 'read the whole paper first'? Well, it matters just as much here. Because, if you get it wrong, it'll be your fault no matter how unhelpful the enquirer has been. You are the professional, remember, and the enquirer is the amateur.

Just think of all the different types of enquirer you might meet, and the things that could go wrong as a result . . .

Type 1: The homophone victim

I'm looking for information on migration patterns in whales

means:

I'm looking for information on migration patterns in Wales

Type 2: The Chinese whisperer

I'm trying to find a song called 'When I would sing under the ocean'

means:

I'm trying to find a song called 'When I was king of the Beotians'

Type 3: The malapropist

Do you have the Electrical Register?

means:

Do you have the electoral register?

Type 4: The generalist

Do you have any books on retailing?

means:

What is Marks & Spencer's current pretax profit?

Type 5: The know-all

I need some statistics from Employment gazette.

means:

I need earnings data for female employees in Croydon; I'm guessing that they're in Employment gazette *because I don't want to seem ignorant.* [Actually, they aren't. And it hasn't been called *Employment gazette* for years, but *Labour market trends*.]

Type 6: The muddler

Have you got any books on Kew Gardens? That's to say, something on the Crystal Palace, if you can manage it. What would be really helpful, actually, would be the index to the Illustrated London news. *Or, better still, a book on tropical fish.*

means:

I'm doing a project on the Westminster Aquarium.

Type 7: The obsessively secretive

Where's the catalogue?

means (after a lot of tactful questioning):

I know there have been reports in the papers that MPs have been accepting cash in return for asking Parliamentary questions, and that one paper has actually named names; I'm very concerned about this because my brother is an MP and he may be involved because he's been asking questions about immigration quotas and he's sponsored by the Strong & Moral Britain Association, which I think is associated with neo-fascist organizations; can you confirm this, or let me know where its funding comes from? I really need to know because I'm about to become a governor of a school with a large number of Asian children – so I'd also like to find out what obligation there is on school governors to declare other interests, but I don't want to approach the school directly about this in case they start asking awkward questions.

3

Most of these are real examples, some exaggerations. (The last one is almost a total fiction.) But they all pose real dangers. Rule number one of enquiry answering is that people almost never ask the question they really want to know the answer to.

Disgruntled and unconvinced enquirers

There are all sorts of reasons for this. They may not want to bother the busy staff. It's true, a big public or educational library can be a busy place. You can have people queuing up at the enquiry desk just when Maisie decides to go off for coffee. When you're under pressure, it's always a temptation to take an enquiry at face value and answer the question actually put to you. Resist it! You're almost certain to have a disgruntled customer returning to the enquiry desk before too long, and that's a waste of everybody's time, and really bad customer relations.

Equally alarming is the kind of enquirer who lacks confidence in your ability to answer the question. They'd sooner browse themselves, perhaps inefficiently, than risk having their time wasted by you. This kind should be sending alarm signals both to you and to your boss. It probably means that the enquirer has had bad experiences before – either with your service or somewhere else. Either way, it's up to you to convince them, quickly, that you can help, even if you don't know anything about the subject they are interested in. This doesn't mean trying to pull the wool over their eyes – that's the worst possible tactic. You're bound to get found out, and you'll just reinforce the enquirer's scepticism. There are ways of being helpful, even if you haven't a clue what the enquirer is talking about.

Secretive enquirers and time-wasters

Then there are enquirers who just don't want anyone to know what they're doing. These can be the most infuriating kind. Despite your gentle persuasion, they resolutely refuse to disclose any information that might help you to help them. But you must suppress your urge to get annoyed. That will only make matters worse. They may have excellent reasons for not wanting to give anything away. It might be someone applying for a job with a big local firm who doesn't want their current

4

employer to get wind of it. It might be an academic who doesn't want to be beaten to publication by a rival. Or would *you* want everyone to know that you were looking for addresses of HIV clinics?

Finally, there are time wasters – people who want to burden you with every tiny detail of their investigation, together with the complete life stories of all their sisters, cousins and aunts. Genealogical enquirers frequently fall into this category. You owe it to your other enquirers to steer this type to the point as quickly as possible. They'll try to persuade you that you can't possibly help them without a full understanding of their needs. They may genuinely believe this, or they may simply have time on their hands, and be looking for someone to talk to. Either way, you have to focus them, tactfully.

There are ways of dealing with all these types. You'll need to be approachable, reassuring, discreet and tactful. This is relatively easy to do face-to-face, more difficult on the phone, because you're not giving the enquirer any visual clues. One thing that does work is to smile when you're on the phone; it can work wonders with a suspicious or hostile enquirer! What you really do need to do, though, is to maintain what the police used to call an attitude of 'suspicious alertness'. You have to find out what you need to know by asking questions, and there are several different questioning techniques that you can employ. This is sometimes rather pretentiously referred to as 'the reference interview', but that implies a formality about the process that can be off-putting for the enquirer. It's really just a structured conversation, directed by you.

Asking the right questions

One of the most useful things you can learn to do in enquiry work is to get into the habit of always asking a supplementary question. Practise it in conversation until it becomes second nature. It can provide an enormous number of clues as to what your enquirer really wants – and can sometimes reveal something completely unexpected that can prevent you from darting off in the wrong direction. Here's a silly example – you're in the kitchen and you think your partner said, 'Have you got the time?' So you reply, 'Do you mean what time is it now or how long does it take to cook?' 'No, no,' your partner answers, 'Did you remember to buy the thyme?'

It's probably second nature to ask a supplementary question in conversation – face-to-face or on the phone – but you should also do it if at all possible with written enquiries as well. This can admittedly be awkward and time-consuming if you are responding to a fax or letter. But with the increasing proportion of enquiries that come in by e-mail, it's easy; you should look carefully at the wording and respond immediately, asking questions that will help you to help your enquirer better.

You need different kinds of questions for different situations, different techniques for dealing with each of the types of enquirer listed above. Let's run through them, and the situations in which you might use them.

Open questions

These invite the enquirer to supply further details without your specifying what additional information would be helpful. You might need to use an open question to deal with a type 4 enquirer (the generalist). Perhaps something like 'Are you interested in any particular aspect of retailing?' And it may be your only way forward with type 7 (the obsessively secretive) with a response like 'I could give you a hand if you can give me an idea of what subject you're interested in.' However, open questions do have the disadvantage of leaving far too many options open.

Closed questions

These force the enquirer to give you a yes/no answer. With type 5 (the know-all) you might be tempted to ask, 'Are you sure that the statistics you want are published there?' But, if the know-all runs true to type, the answer will undoubtedly be 'Yes,' and you will have learned nothing. So you should use closed questions only when you are certain what the options are. For example, you could ask type 3 (the malapropist) 'Do you want the current register for this area?' (see below – 'Who, What, When, Where, Why, How?').

Forced choice questions

These force the enquirer to choose between alternatives. The little kitchen sink drama above uses a forced choice question. Or you might ask a type 1 enquirer (the homophone victim), 'Do you mean the sea creatures or the country?' Forced choice questions can be very helpful – they immediately narrow the field in a way that is being firmly directed by you. But you have to learn to think quickly to come up with two really useful options. You sometimes have to be tactful with forced choice questions too. After all, it's perfectly clear to the enquirer what they want!

Multiple questions

These offer the enquirer a range of options to choose from. You'd use a multiple question when you're really not sure at all what the enquirer wants and you need to fish for ideas. An alternative might be to use an open question, but multiple-choice questions are likely to be much more useful, provided you can think quickly enough to come up with some sensible options. Instead of using an open question for type 4 (the generalist), you could try, 'Are you looking for information on retail management, shop design or location, market research, special types of retailer such as food or electrical goods shops – or even one particular retailer?' The only real problem with multiple questions is that you might confuse the enquirer by offering too many options. So it's worth considering asking a succession of forced-choice questions instead, moving from the general to the particular.

Leading questions

These lead the enquirer in the direction of the answer you want. You should only use them when you're 99% certain you do know what the enquirer wants. They can be dangerous, because they impose your assumptions on the enquirer's request, when what you really need to be sure of is that you haven't made any false assumptions. With type 1 (the homophone victim), you might ask, 'So it's *statistics* on their movements that you're looking for then?' Your enquirer might answer 'Yes', and be quite right. But you still don't know whether it's 'whales' or 'Wales'.

Hypothetical questions

These attempt to glean further information by putting a hypothetical situation to the enquirer. As with the multiple questions, you have to be able to think on your feet to come up quickly with a sensible hypothetical question. But they might be your only hope with type 6 (the muddler), because there is one hypothetical technique that allows you to ask *the* forbidden question. You're never allowed to ask 'What do you *really* want?' That sounds aggressive and suspicious and sends out the wrong signals to the enquirer. But you can put the same question in a hypothetical form by asking 'What would your ideal answer look like?' (Whether or not you ask a hypothetical question of your enquirer, this is one absolutely vital hypothetical question that you must ask yourself. We'll come back to it in Chapter 3.)

Agreeing the task

Whichever questioning technique you employ, the aim is the same. It's to find out, beyond any doubt, exactly what your enquirer wants you to do for them. For this you must be in full possession of the facts. Your chosen questioning strategy should allow you to do one or both of two things – funnelling and probing.

Funnelling focuses the enquirer in from the general to the particular. It would probably help with types 4 (the generalist) and 6 (the muddler). However it can also be an efficient way of dealing with the ambiguities offered by types 1 (the homophone victim), and 5 (the know-all). It's usually the easier of the two techniques to apply because it needn't sound over inquisitive or threatening. Closed, forced choice and leading questions are all suitable for funnelling operations – although you should bear in mind that each of these techniques carries its own hazards. Forced choice is almost always the most efficient one.

Probing seeks further details from the enquirer when you're not at all clear what they want; you would use the technique to try to find out the context in which the enquirer was thinking. It might help you with types 2 (the Chinese whisperer) or 4 (the generalist), and you'll certainly need to deploy this technique with type 7 (the obsessively secretive). But you have to exercise caution and tact when using it, because it can sound inquisitorial. Open, multiple and hypothetical questions might all help you to probe. On the whole, multiple questions are probably best here – they don't sound so inquisitorial, they show that you're trying to help and taking the enquiry seriously, and they're more likely to put the enquirer at their ease than on their guard.

Who, what, when, where, why, how?

'I keep six honest serving men – they taught me all I knew,' said Rudyard Kipling in the *Just so* stories. To answer any enquiry effectively, you need them too; they are the six questions – Who? What? When? Where? Why? How? Your enquirer will fill in some of the blanks relatively unprompted – once you've discovered what they really want, of course, as opposed to what they began by asking. Your supplementary questioning should either fill in or eliminate the others. The first four – Who? What? When? Where? – should provide essential information to enable you to answer the enquiry. The last two – Why? How? – could provide supplementary details that enable you to understand the subject of the enquiry better. You should try to get answers to all six.

➤ Who? *means* Who are you interested in? (This could be a person, an animal, an organization, a civilization, a society, a movement.)
➤ What? *means* What are they doing that interests you?
➤ When? *means* Are we dealing with current, recent or historical information?
➤ Where? *means* Which localities, regions or countries do we have to consider?
➤ Why? *might mean* Why are they doing the thing you're interested in? *or could mean* Why are you, the enquirer, interested in this subject?
➤ How? *might mean* What methods are they using to do it? *or could mean* How do you, the enquirer, want the subject handled?

You wouldn't necessarily always take the questions in this order. (Kipling didn't.) Your enquirer's answers would fill in the blanks for some of them as you went along. Sometimes your questions will seek to elicit more information about the subject that the enquirer is interested in, and at other times you will be looking for information on why the enquirer is interested and how they want the subject handled.

Let's see how it might work for the questions to which our enquirers really wanted answers.

Type 1: The homophone victim

I'm looking for information on migration patterns in whales

> So we need something like a big animal encyclopaedia then? (**Who** are we looking for?)
>
> Oh, sorry – you mean people in Wales moving around? (**What** are they doing?)
>
> Do you mean things like how they travel to work, or what they do when they move house? (**How** are they doing it?)
>
> Is it just movements within the country, or from outside as well? (**Where** do we have to consider?)
>
> Are you looking just for movements now – or back over a period? (**When** do we have to consider?)
>
> Are you looking for information on why people move – or just the figures? (**Why** do you need the information?)

I'm looking for information on migration patterns in Wales

Verdict: Once you've got over the initial misunderstanding, you should be able to get all the way with this enquiry – it's precise and specific.

Type 2: The Chinese whisperer

I'm trying to find a song called 'When I would sing under the ocean'

> Right; have you any idea who sings it, or who it's written by? (**Who** are we looking for?)
>
> I'm afraid I can't find a song of that title. How did you come to hear of it? (**How** can we take this enquiry forward?)
>
> Oh, you heard it on the radio. Can you remember which station or programme? (**Where** did you hear it?)

Was it a pop song or something more traditional? (**When** might it have been written?)

Oh, so it was a baritone solo and you think it might have come from an opera or musical. (**What** kind of song was it?)

Since it's not showing up in any of our musical sources, perhaps the title's slightly different. Let's think of some other way of identifying it. (**Why** aren't we finding it, when the enquiry seems so straightforward?)

I'm trying to find a song called 'When I was king of the Beotians'

Verdict: OK – so you're not going to get all the way to the right answer by this stage. But several things that emerged during your questioning should help you to understand the challenges you face – particularly the fact that the enquirer discovered the title aurally. This should arouse your 'Chinese whisper' suspicions. Meanwhile you now have lots of ideas for places to try: the radio station that played the song, guides to opera and musicals, even asking the enquirer to hum the tune so you can look it up in a dictionary of musical themes.

Type 3: The malapropist

Do you have the Electrical Register?

I'm sorry, I can't find a directory of that title. Is it electricians you're looking for? (**Who** are you looking for?)

Oh, I beg your pardon, I must have misheard – it's the voters' list you need. The local one? (**Where** are you interested in?)

And I presume you want the current one? (**When** do you want to cover?)

Are you just looking up a specific address, or do you need to browse through? (**What** kind of information do you need to find?)

So you're looking for people with particular surnames. Is this because you're trying to trace someone? (**Why** do you need the information?)

11

There might be other kinds of source we could use as well – online directories, for instance. What form would you like the information in? (**How** do you want the enquiry handled?)

Do you have the electoral register?

Verdict: In this instance, we've probably taken the line of questioning much further than is necessary to answer the enquiry – but it does go to show just how much may lie behind even the most apparently simple request. At the very least you will need to confirm that it is the current register for your local area that the enquirer wants; you shouldn't just assume that it is. And, of course, once you've realized the enquirer's initial mistake, you will need to respond tactfully so as to spare them any embarrassment.

Type 4: The generalist

Do you have any books on retailing?

Yes, plenty – and other kinds of information source as well. Are you interested in retail management, shop design or location, market research, special types of retailer such as food or electrical goods shops – or even one particular retailer?' (**Who** are you interested in?)

Ah, so it's Marks & Spencer; are you looking for financial information or news on the company's activities? (**What** do you need to know about them?)

So you need the latest accounts? (**When** are you interested in?)

Just its UK operation, or worldwide? (**Where** do we need to consider?)

Is it detailed information for investment purposes, or just a brief financial profile for information? (**Why** do you need the information?)

Do you need the figures in manipulable form? On a CD-ROM? (**How** do you want the information presented?)

What is Marks & Spencer's current pretax profit?

Verdict: This may be an over optimistic scenario. Enquirers can be extraordinarily sccretive about money matters, and here we reached the crucial company name remarkably fast. After that, however, the thing to bear in mind is that there is an enormous amount of business information available and it's easy to bury an enquirer under a deluge of semi-relevant information. So it's worth probing to find out precisely what they want.

Type 5: The know-all

I need some statistics from Employment Gazette.

I'm afraid I can't find a journal of that title. Can you tell me what specific figures you're looking for and I'll see if I can help you find them somewhere else? (**What** are you looking for?)

I see, so it's statistics on pay. Is it current figures you're after, or something that shows trends over a period? (**When** do you need them for?)

Would that be across all sectors or for a specific group? (**Who** are you looking for?)

So it's female pay. Are you looking for comparisons with male workers as well? (**Why** do you need the information?)

And is it worldwide data, UK, or even a UK region you need? (**Where** do you need the information for?)

Probably the most efficient way to find the figures you need would be online. May I show you a website that would help? (**How** do you want the subject handled?)

I need earnings data for female employees in Croydon; I'm guessing that they're in Employment Gazette *because I don't want to seem ignorant.* [Actually, they aren't. And it hasn't been called *Employment Gazette* for years, but *Labour Market Trends*.]

Verdict: A pretty good funnelling strategy has gone on here. Your immediate offer to help without appearing too inquisitorial starts to elicit the specific information you need to answer the enquiry. Thereafter, you can pin the enquirer down ever more precisely through a succession of questions that demonstrate you're taking the enquiry seriously.

Type 6: The muddler

Have you got any books on Kew Gardens? That's to say, something on the Crystal Palace, if you can manage it. What would be really helpful, actually, would be the index to the Illustrated London News. *Or, better still, a book on tropical fish.*

That's a wide range of topics; is there a common factor? (**Who** (or what subject) are you interested in?)

So it's information on zoos; would it actually be aquariums? (**What** kind of zoos?)

Victorian ones? (**When** would this be?)

And is it particularly London you're interested in? (**Where** are these aquariums?)

Are you trying to do a general history of aquariums? (**Why** do you want the information?)

So you want to concentrate on one aquarium; which one would that be? (**How** do you want the enquiry to proceed?)

I'm doing a project on the Westminster Aquarium.

Verdict: Like type 4, this is probably an over-optimistic scenario. The true muddler would probably go on muddling for some time before giving you the opportunity to start funnelling. But one advantage that muddlers offer over generalists or the obsessively secretive is that they do at least give you plenty of clues.

Type 7: The obsessively secretive

Where's the catalogue?

We have an online catalogue but it only covers the books; can I help further? (**How** can I help you?)

So it's something in the newspapers? (**What** sort of information do you need?)

Do you know roughly when? (**When** should we start looking?)

Can I help you with the website/CD-ROM? What subject are you interested in? (**What** kind of information do you need?)

So it's the cash for questions affair – how would you like me to narrow the search down after that? (**How** would you like the enquiry to proceed?)

Ah, if it's a particular organization you want, a directory might actually help you better, or it might even have a website. (**Who** are you looking for?)

So you actually want something on how it's funded? Well, if it doesn't seem to have a website, let's see if we can find an article on it. (**What** is being done to this organization?)

Is it the race relations aspect you're interested in? For any particular purpose? (**Why** do you need the information?)

So it's school governorships? Sorry, I don't understand the connection with the cash for questions issue. (**Why** do you need to know this?)

It's a family connection? So it's a question of possible conflict of interest? (**How** are the two issues linked?)

So we're looking for something like the rules for school governors? (**How** do you want the subject handled?)

Cash for Parliamentary questions… Strong & Moral Britain Association… neo-fascist organizations… funding… school governors… declarations of interest.

Verdict: Like type 6, this is a somewhat compressed scenario. It would probably take a lot of very tactful questioning to elicit all the aspects of this complex and sensitive affair. Restricting your questioning to sources and techniques, as opposed to the specific information required, will probably reassure your enquirer. Then you can use your demonstration of how the source works to find out more about what your enquirer actually wants.

Keeping good records

As you can see from these examples, some of your questions come out as requests for further information, others as reactions to information received. That's how it usually happens in real life; the responses to either type will help you to fill in more of the blanks. If it's an oral enquiry, or you can respond quickly by e-mail, now is the time to repeat back to your enquirer what you think they want you to do. Which brings us to the question of record-keeping.

Many libraries and information services use enquiry forms; these can be laid out in innumerable different ways and can be printed or electronic. (There's an example on page xii designed especially for the techniques suggested in this book.) They can allow you not only to record the enquiry, but also to list the sources checked and the time taken, collect valuable performance data on the degree of success achieved, and alert your organization to any new information or sources that might be useful to your colleagues in the future. (We'll take a detailed look at this aspect of record keeping in Chapter 9.) For the moment, though, you'll be using the form to ensure that you really do understand what your enquirer wants. Something like . . .

➤ *So we're looking for figures on how people have moved into, out of and within Wales between the 1991 and 2001 Censuses?*
➤ *So we're looking for a song that's a baritone solo that you probably heard on BBC Radio 2 last Sunday, with a title something like 'When I would sing under the ocean?'*
➤ *So we need to browse through the current electoral register for this area?*
➤ *So we just need a single figure – Marks & Spencer's latest pretax profit?*
➤ *So we're trying to find out how earnings for women in Croydon compare with those of men, and whether their situation has improved over the last few years?*
➤ *So we're looking for anything we can find on the Westminster Aquarium, which was demolished some time in the late nineteenth or early twentieth century?*
➤ *So we need: something on the funding of the Strong & Moral Britain Association; information on whatever rules affect school governors; and it*

would help to have something from the papers on the cash-for-questions affair?

Note the use of the word 'we'. This is your problem now, as well as your enquirer's, and it is only good customer relations to make that clear by involving yourself in it.

Finding out how long you've got

Finally, you have to agree a deadline. Often, this will be 'now'. The enquirer will be standing there, and they'll want you to point them in the right direction straight away. (We'll deal with techniques for thinking on your feet in Chapter 3.) But, if the enquiry has come in by phone, email, fax or letter, you need to be quite clear when the answer is required by. So don't take 'As soon as possible' or 'It's urgent' for an answer. 'As soon as possible' could mean next year, from your point of view, and urgency can be measured in minutes or days. So politely pin your enquirer down to a date and/or time. And if you think the timescale is unrealistically short, don't say 'Can't be done' – keep it positive. Explain that you will only be able to provide a limited answer in that time, and invite your enquirer to extend the deadline. More often than not, you'll find that they're able to give you more time. (We'll deal with meeting deadlines in Chapter 6.)

Coming next – not too little, not too much...

You now have nearly all the information you need to tackle the enquiry. But you still have to find out just one more thing – how much information your enquirer wants, and in what detail. Until comparatively recently, information on many topics was a scarce commodity. But increasingly now we're facing information overload, so whereas in the past it may simply have been a question of giving your enquirer whatever you could find, now you must have the courage to select and reject.

Information overload is such an important topic that we're going to devote an entire chapter to it. So in Chapter 2, we'll look at how to provide the right amount of information – not too little, not too much.

To recap . . .

➤ Beware of the pitfalls presented by homophone victims, Chinese whisperers, malapropists, generalists, know-alls, muddlers and the obsessively secretive.

➤ Employ open, closed, forced choice, multiple, leading or hypothetical questions, as appropriate.

➤ Look for answers to the questions Who? What? When? Where? Why? How?

➤ Don't accept a vague deadline.

Chapter 2
Not too much, now
Too much information is as bad as too little

In this chapter you'll find out how to:

➤ recognize the dangers of information overload
➤ discover how much information your enquirer needs
➤ work out the level of specialism
➤ begin earmarking and eliminating potential sources.

There was once a little girl who was given a book to read as a homework project. At the end she had to write a report saying what she thought of it. So she did. She wrote 'This book tells me more than I wanted to know about penguins.'

Bear those penguins in mind as we move to the next stage of successful enquiry answering. First of all, remember a key lesson from Chapter 1 – are they Antarctic sea birds, paperback books or chocolate biscuits? But what really matters, here, is the lesson about 'more than I wanted to know'. If you think that finding information is hard, then rejecting it is even harder. It takes a lot of confidence to say to yourself, 'Now I've found it I realize I don't need it even though it's relevant.' There is always the nagging fear that you might be rejecting the one piece of information that your enquirer would have leapt at as the answer to all their problems. Of course, this shouldn't happen if you've done your questioning properly because, as well as discovering exactly what information is needed, you should also have discovered how much, and at what level.

Only a few years ago, this wasn't an issue. In many cases, you found whatever there was to find in the one or two printed sources available to you, handed them over, and the enquirer probably then had the job of modifying their demands in the light of whatever you had been able to come up with. But the computer has changed all that. All of a sudden we've gone from a situation where information was a scarce resource, to be husbanded and cropped carefully, to a glut, in which it grows and reproduces almost unchecked, threatening to overwhelm us in an impenetrable jungle. There's a phrase for this – information overload.

Information overload

Twenty years ago, if you wanted to find a piece of information that you thought had been in the newspapers, there was really only one place you could go – *The Times Index*. Assuming that you were able to negotiate the somewhat eccentric indexing of our great newspaper of record successfully, you then had the option of actually looking up the story in *The Times* (probably on microfilm, a severe delaying factor in itself) or taking the dates as a basis and scanning through other newspapers for coverage of the same issue. *The Times Index* came out several times a year – very late – and cumulated only into comparatively short periods, so unless you had a pretty clear idea of the dates you needed, you could easily consume the whole time allotted to your enquiry using this one retrieval tool only and still fail to find the information.

There were some alternative sources you could try. The indexing of *Keesing's Contemporary Archives* (now *Keesing's Record of World Events*) was somewhat more efficient, and it cumulated more quickly. But *Keesing's* is an international source, containing far less information than a run of newspapers covering the same period. So if the story you were looking for covered a United Kingdom issue of comparatively little international importance, then *Keesing's* probably wouldn't help. You could also have tried *British Humanities Index* or what was then called *British Technology Index* (now *Abstracts in New Technologies and Engineering*) if you thought the issue might have been the subject of comment in contemporary journals. But both of these sources were highly selective in their coverage of the titles they indexed. By and large, therefore, your chances of failing to find the answer were pretty high.

Multiple media

Now just think how all that has changed. If you're searching for information in the newspapers now, you're more likely to be using a website or CD-ROM than a printed index. CD-ROM versions of newspapers each cover only a fairly limited period – perhaps a year or so. But if you're not sure of your dates, you can use a more general news source such as the BBC News website (http://news.bbc.co.uk) for brief coverage to help you locate the period accurately. Virtually all newspapers now have their own websites, giving access to recent stories and (sometimes for a price) to an archive as well – ft.com is probably the best known. Rolls-Royce services, such as Factiva, LexisNexis or Dialog Profound will allow you to do precise, complex searches on newspapers, wire services and articles for years back.

Of course, Rolls-Royces don't come cheap, but the web does, and that contains an almost unstoppable slurry of information, good and useless. This can sometimes lead people to think that they don't need library and information professionals any more – Google will find it all, they believe. It's certainly true to say that, whereas a few years ago you'd be lucky to find *anything* on most subjects, you now have the potential chance of finding *everything*. But 'everything' is almost certainly too much.

How much does your enquirer need?

So the last stage in your questioning is to find out more or less how much information your enquirer needs. A few years ago, 'Whatever you can find' was often the only realistic option. Now it's increasingly the *least* realistic one. You have the tools to bombard your enquirers with information, but you're not helping them if you do that, because they're looking to you not only to find the information they need but also to filter it, so that they end up with just enough to do whatever they want to do – no more, no less. To help them achieve this, you need to employ the same questioning techniques that we discussed in Chapter 1, and several question types will do.

You could simply ask an open question – 'How much information do you need?' But you might not get a very precise answer – 'Whatever you can find' doesn't really help you very much. Also some enquirers might feel daunted by the task of trying to imagine for themselves what the final answer might look like. That's your job – and we're going to return to it in some detail in Chapter 3. So a multiple question might be better – something like 'Do you just want a few main points in note form, or a page or so of information, or something like an article, or a complete book?' This of course assumes that you have a fair idea of the form in which the information is likely to appear. But if it's a highly technical subject, or the enquirer has used terminology that is unfamiliar to you, you might not know what to expect. So a third possibility might be to put the hypothetical question 'What would your ideal answer look like?' This again puts the onus back on the enquirer, so it's to be avoided if at all possible. But it may be your only hope if your enquirer has really taken you into totally unfamiliar territory. (Whether or not you ask the *enquirer* this question, it's an absolutely crucial one that you need to ask *yourself* – as we shall see in Chapter 3.)

Whatever the enquirer answers – and, in this case, the multiple question is likely to elicit the most helpful answer, from your point of view – you should now have a clear idea of the kinds of sources to go to first. It may seem obvious, but it is vitally important to go to the best source first. (We'll deal with sources in the next couple of chapters.) If it gives you the answer you want then you can, quite simply, stop looking. It doesn't matter if there's more information to be found elsewhere; once you have found enough to satisfy your enquirer's needs you should stop. This isn't being lazy – it's practical.

Information for a purpose

Firstly, once you've found enough to meet one enquirer's needs, you can move on to the next one. That way, no-one is kept waiting longer than they have to be. Secondly, people rarely want information merely to satisfy their curiosity – they almost always need it for a purpose. Let's think about two of the commonest – school or college projects, and retirement hobbies.

However much you may privately regret a student's lack of curiosity, or deplore the narrow focus of a curriculum that forces this attitude upon them, you have to be realistic about it. You're not helping the hapless student or school child at all if you don't take a pragmatic approach. The fact is that they need enough information to allow them to get a good mark, and once they've got that, they can't afford the time to go browsing for more information because they've probably got three or four more projects or homework assignments coming up to deadline too. So help them to find what they want, and then when they've got enough – stop.

Retirement hobbyists, on the other hand, may be operating at the opposite extreme. They're delighted with every additional snippet of detail you can provide – even if they've read it in half a dozen other sources already. The danger here, of course, is that – in the nicest possible way – they can be terrible time-wasters. Whether you actually get carried along by their enthusiasm, or simply can't shake them off, you have to be systematic about your choice of sources to help them too – and the order of priority in which you use them. In both these cases, the aim is to help your enquirer become self-sufficient as rapidly as possible – to give them something to read, and get them settled down reading it.

Do-it-yourself?

Finally, you have to know just how much help to give. Teachers and lecturers are notorious at handing out projects with no thought whatsoever for the ease or difficulty of the research involved. You can easily be faced by two children from the same school class, one of whom wants to do a project on dinosaurs and the other on fourteenth-century Byzantine art, where the teacher appears to have given no thought whatever to the possibility that these might not represent tasks of equal difficulty. In these circumstances, you clearly need to get the dinosaur child started quickly, and devote the bulk of your attention to the Byzantine one. The same problems can apply to retirement hobbies, where people have the habit of devoting their declining years to researching the most esoteric topics (frequently family histories) about which the available information is spread very thinly indeed. Either way, the moral for you is clear – you must be able to work out, quickly, what are the most appropriate sources for the job.

Working out the level of specialism

Exactly the same principles apply in working out the level of specialism your enquirer needs. You need both to probe and funnel to find out whether they are looking for information at postgraduate level or are starting from a position of total ignorance. You can use the same sort of questioning strategy as you did above when finding out the level of detail required, but you also have to be both tactful and suspicious. No-one wants to be thought ignorant, and it's only human nature for people to pretend to greater knowledge than they actually have. So you must use the answers to your Who? What? When? Where? Why? How? questions to judge how much your enquirer knows already. Again, this determines the types of source you use – a layperson asking about varicose veins wants *Black's medical dictionary*, but a student doctor probably wants articles from *Lancet*.

There are different *types* as well as *levels* of specialism. An academic and a practitioner might be equally well qualified in their subject. But the academic, about to embark on a piece of original and mould-breaking research, may genuinely need to be aware of everything that has been written about a subject. A practitioner, on the other hand, whose job is to seek a solution to a practical problem, might be perfectly satisfied with just enough information to offer a good spread of options for taking a decision, for making a recommendation or for taking action. Either way, it is up to you to use your crucial questioning techniques to determine exactly the quantity and quality of information your enquirer needs.

Earmarking and eliminating potential sources

We've actually mentioned a few specific sources in this Chapter – *The Times index*, LexisNexis, *Black's medical dictionary*. In reality, though, we haven't reached the sources stage yet. All we've done so far is to discover the subject required, how much information our enquirer wants, and at what level of detail. You may not have a clue yet what actual sources are available to provide the answer you want. But by now you should be able to start forming a judgment on the *kind* of source that will be most helpful. Equally if not more important, you can now start eliminating sources that are less likely to be useful. Remember – it doesn't even matter if these less helpful sources have some of the information you need. Information overload is going to become more of a problem in the immediate future – not less. So you must have the courage to reject information – something which, it has to be said, library and information professionals have not always found easy to do in the past.

Coming next – avoiding panic, thinking on your feet...

Now at last you have all the information you need to actually start hunting for the answer. But where exactly? It's all very well imagining your ideal source, but how do you discover whether such a source exists? And how do you decide what to do first? In Chapter 3, we'll look at techniques for getting started on answering your enquiry.

To recap . . .

➤ Beware of information overload, and be ready to reject both sources and information.

➤ Make sure you find out how much information your enquirer needs for the purposes of their task – too much is as unhelpful as too little.

➤ Find out by tactful questioning what level of specialism is appropriate to your enquirer's needs, bearing in mind that academics and practitioners may have different needs.

➤ Identify the most appropriate types of source for the job, and concentrate on those first.

Chapter 3
Help! My mind's gone blank
Techniques for getting started

> **In this chapter you'll find out how to:**
>
> ➤ imagine what the final answer will look like
> ➤ decide what kinds of source will provide that answer
> ➤ start identifying actual sources.

Let's go back again to your exams. Do you remember how alarming they could be? You'd turn the paper over, look at the questions and struggle to fight down the mounting waves of panic as you realized that you couldn't answer any of them. Within a few seconds, though, you'd start seeing through the actual wording to the topic behind it. 'Oh yes,' you'd say to yourself with relief, 'That's really a question about the Scottish succession, and this one's really about the League of Nations; I can do those.' Well, exactly the same thing can happen with enquiry answering. You've listened carefully to your enquirer. You've asked sensible questions. You know exactly what they want. Now your enquirer is waiting for you to help. And you haven't a clue where to start looking.

Fortunately, there are techniques for dealing with this. All you need is a few seconds' thinking time. You can buy this time with a positive response – something like 'I'm sure I can help; let me just think for a moment where would be the best place to start.' But do you know you can really help? The answer is – yes, always. You may not be able to find the exact answer your enquirer wants. But you can always help.

What will the final answer look like?

So what do you actually do with the thinking time you've just bought? There's a fundamental technique of enquiry answering that you probably need to deploy with every enquiry you ever tackle. Remember that we said in Chapter 1 that there was one hypothetical question that you always had to ask yourself? Well this is where it comes in – and the question is:

What is the final answer going to look like?

What you should try to do to get started on any enquiry is to conjure up a picture in your mind's eye of what the final answer will look like. You can't yet see the fine detail, and you don't know yet whether there is a source that will provide that answer. But you do at least know how the answer will be laid out on the page or screen, and that's half the battle. Let's see how it would work with just some of the questions that our different types of enquirer posed in Chapter 1.

I'm looking for migration patterns in Wales
This is a request for information that will track and measure the movements of people. If it's about measurement then it will have to take the form of figures presented as statistics. However there could be textual commentary on the figures, and they could also be presented as a graph, chart or diagrammatic map.

I'm trying to find a song called 'When I was king of the Beotians'
You're going to find this in a list of song titles or, possibly, musical themes. Additional information you'd expect to find there would probably include the composer, lyricist, and maybe the longer work from which the song came – an opera or musical, perhaps. Because the first word of the title is a common word, it would be helpful if the source you used had some kind of keyword index as well.

What is Marks & Spencer's current pretax profit?
This is about as straightforward an answer to visualize as there can be – it's going to take the form of a single monetary figure, attached to a company name, with a very recent date. The figure may appear on paper, but because this is a business topic, and timeliness is important, you're more likely to find it on a screen.

I'm doing a project on the Westminster Aquarium
So we're looking for information on a Victorian building in London –
not a first-rank one either, like the Crystal Palace (which our muddled
enquirer mentioned). There'll be descriptive text and pictures but,
because it's not a particularly important building, you're probably not
going to find very much about it in any one place.

*Cash for Parliamentary questions… Strong & Moral Britain Association… neo-
fascist organizations… funding… school governors… declarations of interest*
Quite a shopping list of different kinds of information here. If the cash
for questions affair is a hot topic in current affairs right now, then this
could take the form of fast-moving news, perhaps on a screen. For the
association, you need not only neutral information about its activities
but (because it's dubious) also something probing and investigative. The
school governor information is going to take the form of rules, regulations, codes of practice – that sort of thing.

These are by no means the only forms that final answers to enquiries
could take. Other possibilities include technical diagrams, pictures,
original historical records, bibliographies, recordings, multimedia pre-
sentations, even information supplied by a real person. Once you have
used your common sense and a bit of imagination to work out what the
answer will look like, then you can start looking for actual sources,
secure in the knowledge that you're going for the right kind.

What kinds of sources will do the job?

You're making good progress; you've eliminated a good proportion of
your library or information service's resources because you know it's not
going to help you with this enquiry. You're not thrashing round inefficiently, darting off in whatever direction serendipity takes you. You've
remained clear headed and logical and you're well on the way to finding
the right answer – even though you still don't know what actual sources
exist to help you. So let's go back over these enquiries again, to decide
what kinds of sources will provide the answer you now know you need.

I'm looking for migration patterns in Wales
You're looking for **statistics** on the movement of people. The **Census** is the principal source of statistics on people, so that's almost certainly the best place to start and, since there is lots of government statistical data available online, perhaps you can use the **web**. However, if the enquirer wants commentary on these migration patterns, or maps and diagrams that might be worth looking for in a sociology or demographic **textbook** – or possibly in a **journal** produced by the Census-taking authority.

I'm trying to find a song called 'When I was king of the Beotians'
Some kind of **encyclopaedia** or **dictionary** of song titles would be ideal – and preferably one that's well indexed because of the common word at the start of the title. An alternative might be a **catalogue** of scores, sheet music or recordings. There may also be a good **website** of song titles, with an inbuilt search engine, allowing random searching by keywords – but you will need to be sure that it's authoritative and you can trust it. Many radio station **websites** include playlists, so you could try this if you can pin your enquirer down to the actual station, date and approximate time.

What is Marks & Spencer's current pretax profit?
Big companies like Marks & Spencer almost always have a corporate **website**, so that's the obvious first place to look. They also publish glossy **annual reports**, so that's an alternative. Failing that, something that gives information on a lot of companies – such as a company **directory** or **database**. Or perhaps you could use an index or database to search through the business pages of a **newspaper**, looking for news of the company's latest results.

I'm doing a project on the Westminster Aquarium
You're going to need a fairly specialist source – a detailed **textbook** on Victorian architecture, or a specialist **guide** to London's buildings. You're probably going to have to hunt through quite a lot of **indexes** to find anything at all. The whole thing has a distinctly nineteenth century feel to it, so perhaps the enquirer's idea of the *Illustrated London News* is worth following up – if it's got a decent **index.**

Cash for Parliamentary questions... Strong & Moral Britain Association... neo-fascist organizations... funding... school governors... declarations of interest
There's a lot here, so let's take the sources stage by stage.

For the cash for questions affair, you're going to need a really up-to-date news source – a **web-based** one seems the obvious solution. However 'cash for questions' is only one of many ways in which this issue could be described, so you may have to scan through actual **newspapers** rather than relying on an embedded search engine to find the precise phrase. Better still, you could begin by scanning through **political weeklies** to establish the dates clearly, and then go back to the newspapers of those days for the full detail.

Basic information on the association might come from a **directory**, but comment on its more dubious activities is more likely to have appeared as investigative journalism in **newspaper** features or **journal** articles. Because these may have appeared at any time in the past, you need a source that covers a lot of ground quickly – a printed journals **index** would be cheap to use but could be time-consuming, so you may need to resort to an **online database** of articles.

The rules for school governors sound pretty specialist; some kind of **encyclopaedia** of education law might help, but maybe you'll have to refer your enquirer to a specialist education **information service** or **library**. However, common sense would suggest that there are bound to be **guidelines**, produced by the Government specially for school governors. They're probably free, and very likely available on the **web**. Alternatively you could try the relevant **government department** or even your own **local education authority**.

Identifying actual sources

So now at last we've reached the really hard part – trying to discover whether any actual sources exist that meet your ideal. This is the really daunting bit (isn't it?) – having to learn hundreds of sources and have their details always at your fingertips, so that you can be ready at all times to come out with an instant diagnosis that always seems so impressive when doctors do it. It's true – there are an awful lot of information sources available, and you can spend an entire career answering enquiries and still be discovering new ones on the day you retire. But reassurance is to hand. First of all, successful enquiry work depends on constant daily practice, so the more you do it, the easier it becomes because you can remember more sources without ever having consciously learned them. (Actually this can be a danger as much as an advantage; if you get too used to going to one particular source, you tend to continue using it even if a newer, more efficient one gets published.)

The other reassurance, though, is that you can function perfectly effectively by keeping just a few multi-purpose reference sources in mind. Take a look at the list on page xv of this book – **twenty-five multi-purpose reference sources you can't afford to ignore.** Between them, they will get you started on a very high proportion of the enquiries you will encounter. They are only a start, of course, and many information professionals would dispute some of the choices and want to substitute alternative candidates of their own. Nevertheless, what these sources (or others like them) can do is set you on the track of other, more specialized sources that you can't possibly be expected to remember. So the basic principle is to get to know a limited number of your most useful local sources (UK ones, in the case of the titles listed here) and bear in mind that there is probably an international equivalent – frequently (but not always) American.

Learning some basic sources

There's no great mystery to learning a good range of basic sources. If you're working in a public reference or educational library, it will already be well stocked with sources of this kind, and you can spend some time profitably in the early stages of your new job browsing through some of them to see what they can do for you. Two tips – concentrate first on the ones that are shelved behind the enquiry desk. They will be the ones that your more experienced colleagues have found the most useful over the years. And, secondly, when you are examining and evaluating an unfamiliar source, don't just flick through it at random, but make it do something for you. If it's a directory or a statistical journal, look up a specific organization or figure. If it's an encyclopaedia, follow up all the index references to a subject of your choice. If it's a database, give it a really complex task to perform and see how quickly it responds and how relevant its answers are.

Also behind the enquiry desk you may well find an information file, compiled by the staff – the fruit of years of accumulated collective experience of enquiry answering. Such files can be a goldmine of hard-to-find information, once tracked down never forgotten. It could be a simple card index, or a database on a PC or on the network, or even a set of bookmarked favourite websites. Whatever form it takes, it will be well worth getting to know in detail, because it will be uniquely tailored to your own organization's information specialities and the kinds of questions your enquirers are in the habit of asking. (We'll return to FAQ files in Chapter 9.)

But what if you are operating on your own, with sole responsibility for the library or information service of a specialist organization and no-one to turn to for help? Then you should award yourself an afternoon off, go to your nearest large public reference library armed with the list of sources at the front of this book, and ask to see them. Then use them to find out which journals, directories, statistical serials, websites and databases will help you in your work.

Coming next – focus, dynamism, complexity...

Until comparatively recently, once you'd identified which sources would provide the answer you were home and dry. It was then just a question of looking it up, and handing the answer over. Nowadays, though, life isn't quite so simple. Increasingly, you have a choice not only of source, but also of delivery medium, and you'll also encounter the same information source in several different media – print, magnetic disc, CD-ROM, online. Each medium raises different implications for timeliness, user-friendliness, flexibility, cost. So in Chapter 4, we'll think about the different media you could use, and the advantages and disadvantages that each offers.

To recap . . .

➤ Remember that there are techniques you can learn for stopping your mind from going blank – without having to know any actual sources.

➤ Begin by visualizing the final answer in your mind's eye – a long or short piece of continuous text, a list, table, diagram, picture, map, image on a screen.

➤ Then think what kinds of source will provide this answer – textbooks, journals, statistical serials, directories, databases.

➤ Finally start looking for specific sources, bearing in mind that you will only ever have to learn a small number of multi-purpose reference sources in order to begin tackling most enquiries.

Chapter 4
More on choosing sources
How to decide which is the best medium for the job

In this chapter you'll find out how to:

➤ determine the focus, dynamism and complexity of any subject
➤ compare the merits of printed sources, portable databases and online services
➤ apply these principles to specific enquiries.

Back in the 1970s, when the people currently in charge of library and information services were doing their own professional training, their lecturers used to talk with Messianic glee of a future time when commuters would sit on the train, equipped not with a daily newspaper but with a portable microfiche reader. Absurd as it seems now, it was a fairly respectable theory 30 years ago – and maybe we still haven't learned the lessons it offers. To judge from the newspapers nowadays, you'd think that information retrieval had only just been discovered, and that the only way to do it was by means of computers.

Make no mistake – computers are a vital tool of enquiry work, and they are going to become ever more important as electronic media progressively replace many kinds of printed sources, for reasons of cost if for no other. As more and more high value information appears online, so the web will become an even more important medium. There is a persuasive argument which says that reference libraries should cut down on buying books (which cost a fraction in real terms of what they did when the public library service started) and concentrate instead on high capital cost online and CD-ROM sources which individuals can't afford.

The paperless office?

But the fact is that ink on paper is still a uniquely valuable medium, and we should be very cautious about predicting its demise, because forecasts like that almost invariably come to grief. It's not yet convenient to take an online service on a train or read it in the bath (although with the growth in wireless applications it very soon will be). And screen-based media still don't match the flexibility you can achieve by spreading open publications out on a desk, marking their pages, arranging them in piles. The name chosen for the world's most important computer operating system is very telling. After all, who wants to look at something through a Window when they can handle the real thing?

So, as well as deciding what the information your enquirer needs will look like, you also have to determine certain of its other characteristics before you can decide which medium to use.

Focus, dynamism, complexity

Faced with similar information available in a range of different media, you have to take decisions on which medium would be most appropriate for the job in hand. This involves deciding, for example, whether the information is fast-moving or hasn't changed for a long time, and whether it's about a single topic or is actually about how one issue impinges on another. Let's look at the various types of information you might encounter, and think about the types of source best able provide it.

Focus: broad-based and comprehensive versus narrow and specific

We've already considered the dangers when an enquirer says 'Get me everything you've got on . . .'. It's very unlikely that they literally mean 'everything'. But sometimes people really do want a broad overview of a subject. They might be gathering background information as a preliminary to a more detailed study, or they may just be wanting to brief themselves for a meeting, interview or short-term project. For **broad-based, comprehensive** information, you could use:

➤ an entry in a general encyclopaedia (printed or electronic),
➤ a chapter in a textbook,
➤ a complete textbook.

But if your enquirer has got beyond that stage, and is delving into a subject for more **narrow and specific** detail, you could try:

➤ an entry in a special encyclopaedia (printed or electronic),
➤ an index entry in a textbook,
➤ a report from a specialist organization (i.e. not a conventional publisher),
➤ a journal article (printed or electronic),
➤ a table in a statistical journal (printed or electronic),
➤ an entry in a directory (printed or electronic),
➤ a database record (portable or online).

Dynamism: static versus dynamic

Static information is complete – finished. It's a matter of history. That's not to say that new research won't be done into it in the future but, to qualify as static, the subject must have reached a full stop at the time your enquirer asks you about it. Deciding that information is static is a hazardous undertaking. Stonehenge may be thousands of years old, but *History Today* magazine might still have carried an article in its latest issue on new archaeological finds that tell us more about its purpose or method of construction. But, assuming that you are certain that the information you are being asked about really *is* static, the types of source you could use include:

➤ an encyclopaedia or dictionary (printed or electronic),
➤ a textbook,
➤ a selection of journal articles (printed or electronic),
➤ a statistical time series (printed or electronic),
➤ a directory (printed or electronic),
➤ a CD-ROM database.

With **dynamic information,** you can't rely on sources of the type shown above because you can't be certain that they will reflect the latest state of affairs. Nevertheless, there are degrees of dynamism; a weekly source may well be sufficient for keeping up to date with medical research, papers for which are frequently submitted months before publication. Stock market prices, on the other hand, can change second by second. Bearing in mind these variations, the kinds of source you could use for dynamic information include:

➤ current newspapers,
➤ recent journals,
➤ latest statistical journals,
➤ press releases,
➤ online databases (historical or real-time),
➤ web-based news services,
➤ teletext (broadcast screen-based current information),
➤ audiotex (constantly updated telephone recordings).

One thing you may well find yourself having to do with dynamic information is **browsing** and **scanning.** There may just not be a sufficiently up-to-date index or searchable database for your purposes; or, if there is, you may not be able to afford to use it. So you might have no alternative but to read quickly through quite a lot of text – a selection of newspaper stories, perhaps, or a set of database records. (We'll look at rapid reading techniques in Chapter 5.)

Complexity: single-issue versus multi-faceted

Single-issue enquiries can almost always be summed up in a word or two or a short phrase – 'shopping centres' or 'town planning law'. That doesn't necessarily mean, however, that information on them is going to be easy to find; you might be looking for rare occurrences of a single word or phrase buried in a mass of text. Nevertheless, for single-issue enquiries you might use:

➤ printed sources (if easy to find),
➤ searchable CD-ROMs, or specialist online databases, or the web (if hard to find).

Multi-faceted subjects, on the other hand, are concerned with the impact of one issue upon another – something like 'the planning law implications of non-retail uses of shops in conservation areas'. Fully searchable databases are ideal for multi-faceted subjects; their strength lies in their ability to make and break connections between disparate subjects almost instantaneously. Beware, however – not all databases can do this; web-based news services are built for speed of updating, not searchability, and web search engines don't usually allow you to build searches progressively, in the way you can with professional online services like Lexis-Nexis. So before you decide to use a database to answer a multi-faceted enquiry, make sure that it really *is* fully searchable. Having said that, your chosen database could be a:

➤ portable database – e.g. on a CD-ROM or floppy disk – (if the information is static), or a
➤ specialist online database or the web (if it's dynamic).

Finally, a word of warning: the focus, dynamism and complexity of any subject will vary according to your perception of it. More often than not, this will depend on the environment in which you work. If you work in a specialist statistical or demographic library, for example, then you'll probably might regard the Welsh migration patterns query as pretty general, whereas someone in an all-purpose reference library would see it as very specific indeed. Also, there are two more types of information we need to consider in this context – information that is not available in-house, and information that is not in a published source at all. We'll return to these in Chapter 7.

Print, portable databases, online

The whole point of taking time to determine a subject's focus, dynamism and complexity is to help you decide which medium would be most appropriate for the job. So before we try this out on some real enquiries, let's review the advantages and disadvantages of each.

➤ **Printed sources** are easy to handle, user-friendly and carry no running costs, so you can hand them over to an enquirer with the minimum of initial help. But they can also be out of date, slow to use if you are hunting for information buried in the text, and inflexible if their indexing doesn't accommodate the approach the enquirer wants to take.

➤ **Portable databases**, whether on CD-ROMs, magnetic disks or even DVDs, can get you to the information fast and can allow for a wide range of approaches to the subject, usually with no running costs. But, although in Windows versions they can be quite easy to use, they do not have the uniform 'look and feel' that a web browser offers, and enquirers might be apprehensive about using them and want you to hold their hand; also, although such sources can be fairly up to date, their carrying capacity is limited, and they can still leave you with the nagging fear that, if you had opted to go online, you might have found much more.

➤ **Online services** (including the web) can be right up to date, as well as being fast and flexible. But you'll need to take a decision on whether to go for a high cost commercial online service, where accuracy and searching flexibility can be guaranteed, or for free websites, where you might be swamped with poor quality information.

The right medium for the job?

So how do these assessments work on the enquiries that our seven enquirers posed in Chapter 1? Let's quickly review them for their focus, dynamism and complexity.

I'm looking for information on migration patterns in Wales
Focus: Depends where you work and what sources you have access to; it's pretty broad-based if you have access to lots of statistical and demographic sources, but narrow and specific if you don't, because the enquirer wants one type of population data only.

Dynamism: Relatively static; censuses tend to be taken only once every 10 years, albeit with more frequent intermediate population estimates.

Complexity: Fairly multi-faceted – although this is a standard census enquiry, it does involve combinations and permutations of people and places.

Verdict: Only one source will really do – the Census; since it's designed to answer precisely this kind of enquiry; the **printed** version may be sufficient, although the **online** version could allow even smaller movements to be identified.

I'm trying to find a song called 'When I was king of the Beotians'

Focus: Narrow and specific; only one answer will do, although the range of sources and media in which you might find it remains quite wide.

Dynamism: Static, presumably – unless it's a brand new song, that is; and if your enquirer is looking for a recording of it then you will need to use an up-to-date source to locate one that's still in the catalogues.

Complexity: Single-issue; one song, one composer, commonly requested information.

Verdict: A **printed** index of song titles should do; unless the enquirer wants a recording, that is, in which case you may then have to use an **online** catalogue to identify one that's currently available.

Do you have the electoral register?

Focus: Narrow and specific to the extent that only one source will do; but you still don't know whether the enquirer wants the local current register; they might need one of 10 years ago from the other end of the country.

Dynamism: Relatively static; electoral registers are revised once a year, but you need to beware of changes around the time the new one is due to appear – and you still don't know whether your enquirer wants the current local register or not.

Complexity: Single-issue, if your enquirer simply wants to check the names at a particular address; but if they want to use it for analytical or market-research purposes, then the locally available printed version won't really help.

Verdict: Only one source will do, but as well as being locally available in

printed form, it's republished **online** in various forms – usually as a high cost credit checking and market research tool – and you need more information before you can hand it over with confidence.

What is Marks & Spencer's current pretax profit?
Focus: Narrow and specific, but the range of sources in which you could find this information remains wide.
Dynamism: Could be very dynamic; the announcement might only have come this morning, or might have been available for months.
Complexity: Single-issue; it's a common, readily available figure.
Verdict: Plenty of **printed** sources will give an answer – financial directories, newspapers and journals; **portable databases** could allow you to do more analysis of the figures at your leisure; however, if it really is only a single figure that's needed, then it seems pointless to look anywhere other than **online** via the company's website. (We'll look at getting the best out of the web in Chapter 5).

I need earnings data for female employees in Croydon
Focus: Narrow and specific; although our know-all did originally demand the wrong source, at least the enquiry is precisely defined.
Dynamism: Fairly static; it's updated on the basis of an annual sample.
Complexity: Multi-faceted but, like the Census data above, this happens to be a multi-faceted approach that the printed publication can accommodate.
Verdict: There's really only one source that will provide this level of detail on earnings; it's widely available in **printed** form, although the **online** version could give you greater flexibility and the ability to manipulate the figures. It would also guarantee that the figures were up to date.

I'm doing a project on the Westminster Aquarium
Focus: Pretty broad-based to the extent that anything you can find will be helpful, so there are lots of potential places you could look; once you start looking, however, you'll be looking for something very narrow and specific.
Dynamism: Static; this Victorian building was pulled down years ago, and was never of the first rank anyway.

Complexity: Single-issue, although information on it is going to be fairly thinly spread among a lot of sources.

Verdict: Not going to be easy to find; you'll have to skim rapidly through the indexes and contents pages of a lot of books (Your muddled enquirer might at least have inadvertently given you a lot of ingenious **printed** sources to try – books on Victorian architecture, fish displays, the *Illustrated London News*); however, since this is likely to be an obscure subject, you may want to check **online** because of its greater searching capabilities. (We'll look at search engines in Chapter 5).

Cash for Parliamentary questions… Strong & Moral Britain Association… neo-fascist organizations… funding… school governors… declarations of interest

Focus: Broad-based and comprehensive? Not really; it's actually a whole range of narrow and specific enquiries.

Dynamism: Pretty dynamic, although variably so; the cash for questions issue could be changing from day to day; with the Association it's difficult to say without checking – the possible neo-fascist connection could be a current issue or might not have been covered for years; rules on school governors are probably subject to fairly regular review to keep up with education policy.

Complexity: Multi-faceted throughout; the press might have handled the cash-for-questions affair in any number of different ways and probably only a searchable database will find them, although if it's very current and your enquirer is sure of the dates, you could scan through current newspapers and journals (using some of the rapid-reading techniques outlined in Chapter 5) or use a newspaper website; you might well need a searchable database too to establish any neo-fascist connections with the association and to locate information on its funding; and finding general information on school governors' duties and obligations might be fairly straightforward, but what the enquirer has actually asked for is very specific information on declarations of interest.

Verdict: This difficult and sensitive enquiry will need a wide range of sources: searchable **databases** (whether **portable** or **online**), as well as **printed** news sources and directories, quite likely the web too, and probably discreet contact with officials; it's going to be time-consuming too. (We'll look at deadlines in Chapter 6.)

By the way, did you notice something? Look back at the Focus category in these seven examples; they're nearly all 'Narrow and specific'. That's how it is in real life; even if an enquirer asks a very broad question, and you decide ultimately to use broad-based sources such as general encyclopaedias or textbooks, they will usually have a more specific reason for asking, and it is on that you must concentrate.

Coming next – searching efficiently and quickly...

Now that we know exactly which sources we're going to use, and the most efficient media for the purpose, we can actually get down to looking things up. In Chapter 5, we'll think about strategies for systematic and efficient searching.

To recap . . .

➤ Distinguish between broad-based and narrow, static and dynamic, single-issue and multi-faceted enquiries.

➤ Remember the relative merits of printed sources, portable databases and online services.

➤ Bear in mind the types of medium best suited to the focus, dynamism and complexity of each enquiry.

Chapter 5
Do I really know what I'm looking for?
Tips for efficient search strategies

In this chapter you'll find out how to:

➤ decide what order to try the sources in
➤ search systematically
➤ change tack if necessary
➤ get the best out of the web
➤ employ rapid reading techniques.

We've spent the last four chapters negotiating a labyrinthine and treacherous maze populated by enquirers who don't know or won't tell you what they want, can't speak the language or know too much for their own good. Faced with agonizing decisions on which turnings to take, we've drawn up a careful map of sources that will stop us going round in circles, enable us to pick out the main route and skillfully avoid the dead ends. So are we finally out of the maze? No chance! We're right in the middle. To get out again, triumphantly bearing the answer, we've got to go through the whole process once more, in reverse.

Why? Because the pitfalls we will encounter while actually doing the searching are exactly the same as the ones we faced when trying to find out what our enquirers wanted in the first place. This time, however, we'll be pitted against indexes that lead you to the right word but the wrong subject, 'see also' references that take you on a circular tour, and databases that resolutely refuse to tell you anything at all. You don't believe it? Wait and see.

Where to search first

First of all, you have to decide which of the sources and media you've identified as likely candidates to try first. Once again, this will depend on decisions you've already taken on the subject, the level of detail and specialism, and the currency and complexity of the subject. Possible options are:

> the most **up-to-date** source
> the one most **relevant** to the subject
> the one most **appropriate** to the task in hand.

Let's see how this might work in practice. We'll have a look again at some of our sample enquiries, for which we've now targeted likely sources.

I'm looking for information on migration patterns in Wales
You already know you're going to use the Census to answer this question. It wins on two of the three counts – it's **relevant** (all about population and their movements) and **appropriate** (you're looking for figures). It's pretty **up-to-date** (2001) but a vast document, with many specialist volumes. So you'll have to decide whether to go for the migration volume or the Wales volumes first. Alternatively, you'll need to consider whether the added flexibility and greater level of geographical detail that an electronic version might offer would justify the extra skill you'll need to deploy in using it. You'll also have to consider where to look for later estimates of population movements since 2001 (more **up-to-date** but less detailed), and whether you need to look for textbooks or journal articles for background commentary on the trends (just as **relevant**, perhaps more up to date, but possibly less **appropriate** because not primarily statistical).

I'm trying to find a song called 'When I was king of the Beotians'
Go for the most **relevant** source first – an encyclopaedia, dictionary or (authoritative) website that lists song titles. They don't necessarily have to be particularly **up-to-date** – unless your enquirer wants to buy a recording, in which case a current catalogue or website will be essential.

What is Marks & Spencer's current pretax profit?
You should really go for an **up-to-date** source first if you can, since you clearly need to be sure you have the latest figure. The most obvious starting point would be to see if the company had a website (we'll look briefly at web searching later in this chapter). Failing that, you could try a company directory that gives financial details; it's a **relevant** and reasonably **appropriate** source, but being **up-to-date** is what really matters here.

I'm doing a project on the Westminster Aquarium
You're going to have to try to find **appropriate** sources here – illustrated books on Victorian architecture or guides to the buildings of London. Being **up-to-date** will be no help at all, and your chances of finding a **relevant** source (a book or article on the Westminster Aquarium itself) are virtually zero.

Cash for Parliamentary questions… Strong & Moral Britain Association… neo-fascist organizations… funding… school governors… declarations of interest
Very difficult to decide what to go for here. You probably need to be **up-to-date** for the cash-for-questions aspect, since the story may still be developing – so use an online news service or scan through the papers themselves. For the Association a searchable database or the web seems the most **appropriate** starting point, since you will need to test speculations about funding and links with neo-fascist organizations; you could save money by starting with a less **up-to-date** CD-ROM, but may have to shift to an online source if the information on the CD-ROM is not of recent date. For the guidance for school governors, the school itself might seem the most **relevant** place to go, but it's hardly **appropriate** since your enquirer doesn't want to alert the school; the more remote Department for Education & Skills or the local education authority are equally **relevant**, and far more **appropriate**.

Searching systematically

Now you've finally decided on your first source, what are you going to search for? Plenty of things can go wrong, and you have to be ready for them. It's all really a matter of common sense, but you must spend a few moments thinking out your strategy. Among the myriad things that can cause problems, these are some that you should certainly consider:

Variant spellings

Whether you're using a conventional index or a database, variant spellings can cause big problems, so try to anticipate them. Proper names are especially tricky; it was Cain who killed Abel, but Kane who had a sled called *Rosebud*. And where on earth do you start looking for the fast food chain that calls itself *Mc*Donalds but calls its culinary *pièce de résistance* a Big *Mac*? Many of the databases, and quite a few of the printed sources, that you use will be American, so you will have to watch out for 'color' instead of 'colour', 'disk' instead of 'disc'. This may not be a great problem with alphabetical indexes; your eye will quickly spot the difference. But, with many databases, you're flying blind, and if you search for 'favourite' or 'labour' they'll keep on giving you a zero result no matter how much you swear at them. There are plenty of other pitfalls with variant spellings in British English – jails can be gaols, choirs can be quires (in more archaic sources anyway) – one could go on but that's enough.

Homonyms

If you're looking for hardware but keep coming up with foodstuffs then you've hit the homonym problem associated with 'nuts', which is equally at home in the two phrases 'nuts & bolts' and 'monkey nuts'. Numismatists studying the indented wax symbols at the base of legal documents run the risk that their hunt for 'seals' will lead them to Arctic sea mammals. And specialists in literacy keep finding themselves being vexingly directed to a large Berkshire town when they look up 'reading'. You need to be particularly alive to the dangers of homonyms, and be ready with tactics for taking evasive action if necessary. It's particularly – but not exclusively – a problem with free-text database searching (including the web). Strategies that you can employ to deal with it include adding a further qualifying term to your search – such as 'numismatics' or 'literacy' – or, in the case of the 'nuts' problem, using a trade classification code (if one is available) instead of the word. In fact, whenever you use a searchable electronic source, do click on any buttons that look as if they might lead to an onboard thesaurus or other searching aid.

British versus American terminology

Many databases, and quite a few really good printed reference sources, are American, so it's important to be aware of American terminology. We all watch Hollywood movies (or do we mean films?), so most people would probably remember to use 'elevator' instead of 'lift', 'streetcar' instead of 'tram' and 'pants' instead of 'trousers' (although this last one presents its own special homonym problems as well). But how many Europeans know that the American for 'central heating' is 'space heating', and is equally unfindable whether you are using a database or a printed index?

Synonymous, broader, narrower and related terms

Really well-constructed indexes are based on a thesaurus which allows for all the different approaches that a searcher could take towards a subject. Alas, however, the real world is full of ineptly constructed indexes. So it's wise to assume that you will have to fend for yourself.

Whether you're using a printed index or a free-text database, you're likely to have jotted down a list of likely words and phrases to search under before you start. That's fine as far as it goes, but with only a little extra effort, you can create a far more valuable searching aid for yourself. So instead of just jotting down those words and phrases randomly, in the order they occur to you, try listing them in a structured way. What you'll be doing is creating your own mini thesaurus – specially designed to help you with your current enquiry. It will minimize your chances of missing something relevant and – just as important – it will help you to avoid wasting your time by accidentally going over the same ground twice.

Let's see how this might work in practice. Suppose you've been asked for information about some aspect of railway management. You might start by randomly jotting down:

train services
commuting
public transport
rail services
surface transport
fixed links
rapid transit

There are some pretty useful words and phrases here, including probably some that you wouldn't initially have thought of for yourself. So how
do you think of suitable words and phrases in the first place? You could
discuss the topic with colleagues, of course, and see what ideas they
come up with. But a really good method when you're working alone is to
start discussing the topic with yourself in your head – or even out loud,
if that makes it any easier. Listen carefully to the words and phrases you
are using when you do this, and note them down as they occur to you.
That will give you the makings of an initial list of search terms. But then
you can add a lot more value to this list by rearranging these terms in
some sort of hierarchy. Going back to look at that random list, you could
start with:

Rail services, train services

These are your **root terms,** the basic words (or, in this case, phrases)
under which you will usually start looking. For all practical purposes,
they're synonymous terms, so you'll need to check under both, since
they will be separated alphabetically in a printed index and, if you're
using a search engine, typing in one of the phrases is unlikely to reveal
information indexed under the other.

Then you need to think of some **broader terms,** for those occasions
when you encounter an index (whether printed or electronic) that isn't
as specific as this. These broader terms go above the root terms, at a

different level of indentation to show their place in the hierarchy. So you might add:

> Public transport, surface transport, fixed links
>   Rail services, train services

Other indexes that you use might be much more detailed, and retrieve far too much information under your broader or even your root terms to be useful. (Remember always to be alive to the dangers of information overload.) So you will also need to think of some more specific, **narrower terms** that meet your enquirer's precise requirements. Perhaps something like:

> Public transport, surface transport, fixed links
>   Rail services, train services
>   Commuting, rapid transit

Once you've been through this little exercise, stick to it when searching and you'll be sure you're making the most efficient use of your time (but see 'Changing tack' below).

Changing tack ('see' and 'see also' references)

It's when things start to go wrong that your careful preparation for searching will really pay off. Hunting for information is a journey into the unknown. Every source you use will be differently constructed, and have its own indexing quirks. As your searching progresses, you're bound to come across relevant words and phrases that you never thought of in the first place, and that's when you'll have to take the difficult decision on whether it's worth going back over sources that you've looked at already.

If you do, your mini-thesaurus should at least help to ensure that you don't merely repeat work that you've already done. Let's go back to those train services; suppose you're onto your third or fourth possible source, and you suddenly find the following entries:

➤Commuting *see* Suburban rail services
➤Rapid transit *see also* Light rail

These entries show two further terms which, in an ideal world, you would have thought of for yourself when you constructed your mini-thesaurus. This 'See' reference should mean that there are *no index entries at all* under 'commuting' (the term you first searched on), and that *all* the entries are under 'suburban rail services' (the indexer's preferred term). With the 'See also' reference, on the other hand, there could be relevant entries under *either* 'rapid transit' *or* 'light rail' because, for the purposes of this index, they're similar but not identical.

These discoveries should prompt you to do two things. Firstly, you must amend your mini-thesaurus. There's no great problem with 'suburban rail services'; it's clearly at the same level of hierarchy as 'commuting'. 'Light rail' is a bit more tricky, though; it's not quite at the 'rapid transit' level, but then it's not quite at the 'rail services' level either. It's a related term, sitting somewhere in between. (It should also prompt you to continue the discussion in your head and come up with the additional term 'trams', which fits in more or less at the same level.) So your mini-thesaurus will now look something like this:

Public transport, surface transport, fixed links
    Rail services, train services
        Commuting, rapid transit, suburban rail services
(Light rail, trams)

The second thing you have to do is decide whether or not to go back over previous sources and recheck them for the new terms. This is where your systematic approach really pays off, because if you do decide to go back to previous sources, you can do so secure in the knowledge that you only have to check under the newly discovered terms, since you can guarantee that you've already searched systematically under the terms you thought of in the first place. If there's nothing extra to be found under the new terms, then you should be able to abandon the source without wasting any more time on it. (We'll discuss efficient management of your time in Chapter 6.)

Searching databases efficiently

Printed indexes will use 'See' and 'See also' references with varying degrees of efficiency and consistency. Databases, on the other hand, can offer a whole range of further searching aids. They may be able to display an alphabetical list of the words and phrases adjacent to the one you've chosen. They might be based on a structured thesaurus, which you can actually call up on screen and examine for possible further search terms. They may employ a hierarchical numeric classification (such as a trade classification) which will automatically retrieve all records classified below the point at which you actually enter. They'll almost certainly allow you to use truncation, so that a search on the term 'rail*' can automatically retrieve 'railway' and 'railroad' (and 'railings', so beware!).

Searching software will frequently return results ranked for relevance (treat this facility with caution, however; the software's idea of what's relevant frequently won't be yours or the enquirer's). Natural language searching, in which the software can actually interpret a phrase like 'Travelling in to work by train', is another possible facility; it can allow you to leave an enquirer searching for themselves while you attend to somebody else. (We'll deal with prioritizing enquiries to make the most efficient use of your time in Chapter 6).

Sometimes an 'advanced search' or 'power search' facility will offer you the option of using Boolean logic. Provided the database you are searching on has been efficiently indexed, this can be a very powerful retrieval tool indeed. Boolean logic works by linking words or phrases together using the logical operators OR, AND and NOT. It works like this:

A search on: apples OR pears   will retrieve every document that mentions apples and every document that mentions pears (including of course documents that mention both).

A search on: apples AND pears   will retrieve only those documents that mention both apples and pears (documents that mention only apples or only pears won't be retrieved).

A search on: apples NOT pears will retrieve documents that mention apples, but not when they also mention pears (and will of course retrieve no documents that mention pears alone either).

There are refinements to Boolean logic, allowing you to specify that words must be adjacent to or within a certain number of words of each other. This lets you search for a phrase such as 'Land of Hope and Glory', ignoring the common (and usually non-retrievable) words in between the important ones. You can also usually bracket groups of words and phrases together, as in:

(apples AND pears) AND (farming OR horticulture) NOT (England OR Wales)

Whatever help is at your disposal with your database searching, you must still be ready to modify your searching strategy in the light of information retrieved – and to do so systematically.

Getting the best out of the web

The enquiry answering capabilities of the world wide web have improved beyond all recognition over the years; it's still not going to be the answer to everything, but it is now probably the single most effective enquiry answering tool available.

Most of our seven enquiries would be worth a try on the web at some stage. Almost all major institutions, and very many tiny ones, have promotional websites, so the web is particularly good at providing information on named organizations. It's therefore the obvious choice for the Marks & Spencer enquiry. It is also a natural home for pressure groups, so an anti-racist organization's site may well yield useful cautionary information about the Strong & Moral Britain Association. It's a great place for enthusiasts to pursue their individual obsessions too, so a quick speculative search for material on the Westminster Aquarium might pay dividends. And, as more and more Government information – particularly statistical data – is published on the web, it's an obvious port of call for the Welsh migration and Croydon earnings queries.

There is now an enormous quantity of high quality information free on the web – from public bodies, from non-governmental organizations such as professional associations or charities, from academic sources and from international organizations. Reputable commercial sites frequently offer some free information as a taster to tempt you to buy more specialized charged-for services; nothing wrong with this, so make the best use you can of the information that is freely available, and take a view on whether you think it's worth purchasing more.

However, as with all the other media you use, do make sure that you are systematic in your web searching; web pages are littered with tempting links to other sites, and if you are induced to follow any, make sure you don't forget what your enquirer's question was in the first place. Bear in mind, too, that there's little if any quality control over many websites, so there's no guarantee that what you find will be authoritative or accurate. So do satisfy yourself that the organization whose site you are using can be trusted; look it up in a reliable directory before committing yourself. After all, the enquirer will blame you – not the website – if you provide inaccurate or biased information.

Finding out what's worth having

So how on earth do you find out what's worth having? Firstly, by using your common sense; if you've heard of the organization whose site you're visiting, and know it to be reputable, then obviously you can take the content of its website on trust. But how can you be sure that it is the organization you think it is? Sometimes internet domain names are not registered by the organization that you would expect to own them but by someone else – maybe for unscrupulous motives. So try firstly using a reputable printed or online directory to find details of organizations that are likely to help (including their web addresses), and then go from there directly to their websites.

There are plenty of sources that will help you find reputable websites; one particularly useful one is Facet Publishing's *The public librarian's guide to the internet* (see page 104). This is actually useful to a far wider range of web users than its title suggests; anyone who wants a good shortlist of high quality sites on a specific topic will find this guide of value. It not only gives details of individual sites, but also of services that provide links to related sites – multidisciplinary subject directories, portals, subject gateways, subject resource guides. Don't regard it as the be-all and end-all, though, because new websites are coming online all the time.

And finally, a cautionary tale. Puzzled by why her phone bill suddenly went up just as her teenage son started to learn the guitar, one mother discovered that, every time he wanted to learn a new chord, he went online and downloaded the correct fingering from a guitar tutor website. Now there are only a limited number of guitar chords, and they don't change; so she took him along to the local music shop and bought him a book – indexed and thumb-tabbed – that showed the lot, with fingering diagrams. Result: he had a universal reference source for his chosen hobby, and her phone bill returned to manageable proportions. Moral: don't regard the web as a universal panacea; there are many kinds of enquiry for which it still isn't the best medium.

Searching with a purpose

Speculative searching probably means using search engines. These index the contents of the millions of web pages available and usually attempt to rank them for relevance. Your web browser will have a button offering links to some of them, and so probably will your internet service provider's home page. You'll discover others by yourself as well. Some of the best known ones are:

- ➤ AltaVista (www.altavista.com)
- ➤ Excite (www.excite.com)
- ➤ Google (www.google.com)
- ➤ InfoSeek (www.infoseek.com)
- ➤ Lycos (www.lycos.com)

➤ Northern Light (www.northernlight.com)
➤ Webcrawler (www.webcrawler.com)

In addition, there are several 'meta' search services, which search the other search engines. They tend to bring back only limited numbers of results, which can save you having to wade through screenfuls of hits, but they don't necessarily allow you to take advantage of the individual search engines' special characteristics. The best known ones are:

➤ Dogpile (www.dogpile.com)
➤ Mamma (www.mamma.com)
➤ Metacrawler (www.metacrawler.com)

A growing number of search engines have UK or other country equivalents – you'll be able to link to these from their main sites, or you could try experimenting by substituting .co.uk for .com. (In some cases, if you go to a search engine site from a UK internet address, then you'll automatically be linked to the UK version of the search engine.) Some have 'power search' facilities, allowing you to use slightly more sophisticated search techniques (such as the Boolean logic outlined above) and hopefully to achieve more precise results. Finally, Yahoo! is a rather special case. It's not strictly a search engine so much as a detailed classification of websites, with different versions for each country. You can find it at:

➤ www.yahoo.com
➤ www.yahoo.co.uk

. . . and so on for other countries.

Whichever search engine you go to, you're likely to find that the window where you type in your search terms is surrounded – almost overwhelmed, sometimes – by vivid and enticing links to other services – news, weather, travel, horoscopes, lonely hearts and much more. This can sometimes be useful, but it's just as likely to be a nuisance if you simply want to do your own searching with no off-putting diversions. At the time of writing, Google is an honourable exception to this rule; its search screen is sparse and uncluttered, and it's also extremely good at producing relevant results. However, there's no particular reason why it need automatically be the search engine of choice. So experiment with them all, ask your colleagues' opinion, and reach your own conclusions.

Even though they each index only a fraction of the web's total content, search engines do still tend to produce vast numbers of hits, and it's not always obvious why some items have been retrieved at all. So it's often more efficient to start with a search engine, but then to follow links as soon as you get to a nearly relevant site. For example, you could try putting in a search that goes something like...

"school governors" (rules regulations guidelines) uk

. . . then pick the most promising result out of the first few (possibly the site of one particular local education authority or school) and follow links from there to the site of an authoritative national institution. Another way – as mentioned above – is to find an organization's web address in a conventional printed source, such as a directory or an advert, and then go online for further details.

Web addresses – have a guess

If you can't find an organization's web address, you can always try guessing it. It doesn't work every time of course, but it's surprising how often it does, with practice. It would certainly be worth trying this technique to see if Marks & Spencer has a site that gives its pretax profit. Some possible guesses might be:

➤ www.marks&spencer.com
➤ www.m&s.co.uk
➤ www.marksandspencer.com
➤ www.marks-and-spencer.com
➤ www.marks_and_spencer.co.uk

If you do guess, you also need to know what domain to try – the bit that indicates the type of organization. These are some of the commonest:

> ➤ .ac or .edu (educational establishments)
> ➤ .co (companies)
> ➤ .com (global commercial sites)
> ➤ .gov (government departments and agencies)
> ➤ .int (international organizations)
> ➤ .mus (museums)
> ➤ .net (network administrative bodies)
> ➤ .org (associations, professional bodies, organizations)
> ➤ .sch (schools)

A few addresses, however, don't include a domain; the British Library's web address, for example, is simply www.bl.uk. United States sites don't have a country code; however other sites do, so this is the last element you need to consider when working out what a web address is likely to be. British sites have .uk and it's not too difficult to work out the rest. Here are a few examples.

> ➤ .au (Australia)
> ➤ .ch (Switzerland)
> ➤ .de (Germany)
> ➤ .fr (France)
> ➤ .nl (Holland)

Using the web like a professional

Although anyone can use the web with very little introduction, it takes skill to use it well. Your job as a professional is to ensure that you can help your enquirers by being able to achieve better search results than they can manage by simply relying on Google. The web is now such a fundamental tool for enquiry answering that it's worth taking some time out to learn how to use it properly. Facet Publishing (the imprint of CILIP: the Chartered Institute of Library and Information Professionals) publishes several titles on internet use – not just the web, which is merely the multimedia part of the net. You'll find details of *The library and information professional's guide to the internet*, *A guide to finding quality information on the internet* and *The public librarian's guide to the internet* in this book's guide to key reference sources (Chapter 10). However, these are just a few of a wide range of books published by Facet on internet and intranet use; you can get details of others by visiting www.facetpublishing.co.uk.

Finally, don't forget to bookmark the useful sites you find and add them to your list of favourites – either temporarily for the purposes of the current enquiry, or permanently as part of your library's useful information file. Be disciplined about arranging your favourites logically too. There's nothing more frustrating than not being able to find the wonderful site you were using only yesterday.

Rapid reading

You can't always rely on printed sources having an index. And, even if there is a suitable online database for your purposes, you may not be able to afford to use it. So there will be times when you find yourself having to scan and browse rapidly through the text of an actual document or web page. You might find yourself having to look at a selection of articles, a set of news headlines, a bulky report or a chapter of an inadequately indexed book. If this happens, you certainly don't have to read every word. There are techniques that you can learn for rapid and efficient reading, and it's a good idea to practise them. Some of the commonest ones are:

> ➤ Look at the document's preliminary matter, bullet points, lists or captions first.
> ➤ Read down the middle of the page, relying on your peripheral vision to spot significant words. (How do you know what those words are going to be? You use your mini-thesaurus.)
> ➤ Alternatively, if you're faced with long lines of print, bounce your eye from the left hand to the right hand side of the page.
> ➤ Look for capitalized words (likely to be the names of organizations or people), and also for abbreviations and numerals; all these will stand out from the rest of the text and offer valuable clues as to the document's content.

> ➤ Read the first sentence of each paragraph. (This is a first rate technique for getting through a long document, such as a report, quickly.)

This isn't really 'rapid reading', of course. You're just reading at your normal reading speed. The trick is knowing what *not* to read. And it only works if you already have a pretty clear idea of what you're looking for. Your eye won't instinctively spot a significant word or phrase unless you've already worked out what those words or phrases are. So constructing your own mini-thesaurus is just as important for browsing and scanning as it is for using indexes. And one final tip: if the text you have to read is on a screen, print it out first. The screen flickers, the lights flicker, and the resolution is probably clearer in print anyway. So give your eyes a break by making it as easy as possible for them to spot what you're looking for.

Coming next – meeting deadlines every time...

All of this searching takes time, and you start out with no guarantee of success. So what do you do when you realize that time is running out and you're no nearer an answer than you were when you started? In Chapter 6, we'll look briefly at efficient time management, which can allow you to meet deadlines every time.

To recap . . .

➤ **Decide whether to go for the most up-to-date, most relevant or most appropriate source first.**

➤ **Construct your own mini-thesaurus before you start searching.**

➤ **Beware of variant spellings, homonyms, and British versus American terminology.**

➤ **Be ready to change your search strategy (and amend your mini-thesaurus) in the light of what you find.**

➤ **Exploit the web – using search tools, following links, guessing web addresses.**

➤ **Learn and practise rapid reading techniques for scanning and browsing.**

Chapter 6
Quick! Time's running out
How to meet deadlines every time

In this chapter you'll find out how to:

➤ **distinguish between vital and urgent tasks**
➤ **establish a working timetable**
➤ **compromise on the answer**
➤ **provide progress reports.**

Ads for online services have a lot to answer for. How many times have you seen or heard phrases like 'A world of information at your fingertips'? The trouble is that enquirers believe them. They really do believe that you can now find anything you want with just a few deft mouse clicks. The web, they think, has it all. You can't really blame them. Internet service providers, electronic publishers and – it has to be said – some incautiously upbeat library and information professionals have all raised their expectations to the point where, as far as they're concerned, the information superhighway is complete down to the last white line.

E-mail and fax haven't helped either. A dozen or more years ago, dealing with written enquiries did at least give you a breathing space, in which you could agree a realistic deadline that allowed you to work out a sensible search strategy including making provision for things going wrong. Nowadays, though, enquirers know that they can have a written answer instantly; blaming delays on the post is no longer an option. Actually there are many positives to this; as we discussed in Chapter 1, e-mail does allow you to maintain that vital dialogue with the enquirer, even if they're on the other side of the world. But there's no doubt that improvements in telecommunications are encouraging enquirers to demand even tighter deadlines.

So what can you do about it? The first thing is to maintain a positive attitude, keep a clear head, and distinguish between what's vital and what's urgent.

Vital versus urgent

We discovered in Chapter 1 that 'urgent' is not an acceptable deadline for any enquiry. You need to know *how* urgent; you need a date and/or a time. Now we need to take that a stage further and make sure that we really understand what we mean by urgency.

Faced with a limited amount of time and a number of competing tasks, you need first of all to sort them into priority order and allocate time between them – and you need to revise that timetable constantly as new tasks come along to demand your attention. To do this, you need to be clear about the relative importance and difficulty of the tasks before you. Let's deal with importance first. A 'vital' task is one without which your organization cannot function. An 'urgent' task is one which has an imminent deadline; it may or may not be vital. If you don't buy information sources, install, catalogue and index them, and learn how they work, then you can't answer the enquiries. So these are 'vital' tasks. But they're not necessarily 'urgent'; if you put them off until tomorrow, no great harm may be done. They may in due course become urgent; if you're constantly being asked for information that's sitting in a document that you haven't yet catalogued, or a piece of software that you haven't yet installed, then that cataloguing or installation becomes not only 'vital' but also 'urgent'. Let's see how it might apply to enquiry work.

First come first served?

You might have three urgent enquiries to do. They all have the same deadline. But one is for a colleague doing a college course on day release, another is for your boss and the third is for a client of your organization. Your job is to answer enquiries for all these three people, so they're all vital; if you don't do them, you'll be in trouble. But if you fail your colleague you'll probably just get ticked off; if you fail the boss you might lose your job, and if you fail the client, everyone might lose their jobs.

So you can see that there are degrees of urgency, depending on how vital the task is. You might deal with it by:

➤ **firstly** suggesting an appropriate source for the colleague to use for him or herself
➤ **secondly** warning the boss that you're doing an enquiry for a client and either providing a brief 'holding' answer for the boss or negotiating a longer deadline (or both), and then…
➤ **thirdly** concentrating on the client.

Once you've dealt with your competing enquiries in the manner outlined above, you can then work out how long you need to allocate to each. Five minutes with the catalogue or a couple of other finding aids may be enough for your college colleague, and 15 minutes looking up and downloading or photocopying a few pieces of information will put the boss on the back burner for a while. This leaves you the rest of the morning to spend doing database searches, scanning journal references and compiling a list of addresses for the client. (And preparing to present the answer in a helpful way; we'll look at adding value in Chapter 8.)

Of course, it doesn't work like this in a busy reference or educational library. There every enquirer is equally important, and you have to employ different techniques to ensure that everyone's deadlines are met. To do this, you really need to be able to assess instantly the relative difficulty of answering each enquiry, and the amount of time you'll need to do it. There's probably no easy way of doing this; it comes with experience and, even then, you'll still encounter some enquiries that turn out to be almost impossible to answer, even though you thought they were going to be easy. But you can help yourself by making sure that you do know your basic reference sources really well – just a strictly limited number of them, such as the ones listed at the front of this book. If you are familiar with their contents, then you should know what's feasible and where you're going to have to negotiate with the enquirer about providing a compromise answer.

Time is money

Difficulty doesn't necessarily equate to time (although it might). An alternative to spending time on a difficult enquiry might be to use a charged-for database, where the time saved justifies the expense. Assuming that you've correctly identified the right one to use, searchable databases can save you an enormous amount of time – not least because they *fail* as quickly as they *succeed*. Just think about it for a moment. If you use printed sources, it takes you longer to fail to find the answer than it does to succeed because, once you've found it, you stop looking. Whereas if you keep not finding it, you go on looking until you've exhausted every possibility. A database, on the other hand, fails as quickly as it succeeds by telling you instantly that there's nothing available on your chosen subject, so you know much further ahead of the deadline that an enquiry is going to be difficult, and you still have time to do something about it.

The moral here is that time is money. Whether you choose to spend pounds on an online search that takes five minutes, or restrict yourself to 'free' printed sources or the web and spend an hour looking things up or surfing instead, the result is the same – cost to your organization. In making efficient use of your time, and deciding when to call a halt and compromise on the answer instead, you must always bear in mind that every minute you spend on an enquiry is costing your organization money. It's not just the cost of your salary either, or the online or copying charges – there are overheads to take into account as well – things like lighting, heating, rent and rates, to say nothing of the cost of acquiring and managing all your information sources in the first place. The less efficiently you plan your search strategy, the more it costs your organization.

Your working timetable

We've already done some assessment of the relative difficulty of our sample enquiries. Assuming that they all have the same deadline (and that your library or information service has all the sources necessary for answering them), let's see what this is likely to mean for our timetabling.

I'm looking for information on migration patterns in Wales
Verdict: A very small quantity of looking up – on the Office for National Statistics website or in a statistical digest – should tell you that the Census is the place to look. But, whether you use it in electronic or printed form, the Census is a huge document. So this enquiry is fairly **easy** but could be a bit **slow**.

I'm trying to find a song called 'When I was king of the Beotians'
Verdict: The trouble with this enquirer's Chinese whisper is that you're starting off looking for something that doesn't exist, and then when you've realized that, you haven't a clue what the real title is. So this enquiry could be **hard** and **slow**. (Of course, once you do know the correct title, then there are plenty of lists and catalogues of songs to check it in; so the final stages will probably turn out to be fairly easy and quite quick).

Do you have the electoral register?
Verdict: It will probably take only a minute or two to check that the enquirer really does want the current register for the local area; assuming they do, and that you're working in a public library, then you'll have it; if you're not, then you'll at least know who to phone to check it. So this enquiry is very **easy**, fairly **quick**.

What is Marks & Spencer's current pretax profit?
Verdict: This enquiry is **easy** because there are plenty of places where the figure could be found, and should be very **quick** if you use the web.

I need earnings data for female employees in Croydon
Verdict: Your enquirer didn't help to start with by suggesting an inappropriate source; but once you've sorted that out, finding the right source should be a fairly simple looking-up job – again perhaps via the ONS website. It may take you a little time to find it there, so this enquiry will eventually turn out to be fairly **easy** but could be a bit **slow**.

I'm doing a project on the Westminster Aquarium
Verdict: Once you've interpreted this enquirer's muddle, you'll probably

find that the answer requires a lot of looking up for not much information. So this one will be **hard** and **slow**.

Cash for Parliamentary questions… Strong & Moral Britain Association… neo-fascist organizations… funding… school governors… declarations of interest
Verdict: This is a very big job; it's probably going to involve looking things up, searching printed and electronic sources and phoning round. You might be able to speed some parts of it up by using databases, but there are so many aspects to it, and some of them are so speculative, that it's still going to take a long time. So it's pretty **hard** and very **slow**.

Finally, then, let's use these assessments to sort the enquiries into priority order, so that everybody gets started as quickly as possible.

1 *What is Marks & Spencer's current pretax profit?* (Very easy, very quick.)
2 *Do you have the electoral register?* (Easy and probably quick.)
3 *I need earnings data for female employees in Croydon.* (Fairly easy, could be slow.)
4 *I'm looking for information on migration patterns in Wales.* (Fairly easy but could well be slow.)
5 *I'm doing a project on the Westminster Aquarium.* (Hard and slow, but at least you can leave the enquirer browsing.)
6 *Cash for Parliamentary questions… Strong & Moral Britain Association… neo-fascist organizations… funding… school governors… declarations of interest.* (Hard and slow, and the enquirer will need a lot of help.)
7 *I'm trying to find a song called* 'When I was King of the Beotians'. (Until you discover the correct title, this is going to be hard and slow and is probably going to require you to do quite a lot of asking around on the enquirer's behalf.)

Beware! This is not the right order for everyone. People's perception of difficulty varies depending on their experience and the environment they work in. (A music librarian might put the 'King of the Beotians' right at the top of the list, for example, because at least they ought to be able to come up with plenty of ideas for tackling it.) So you should take this section as a guide to technique, not as the answer to the problem.

If you're actually doing all the enquiries yourself, your chosen order of priority means that you can start getting answers out from the earliest possible moment. If you're simply helping the enquirers to find the answers for themselves, then this strategy means that everyone gets started as rapidly as possible and you have time to monitor everybody's progress and help wherever necessary.

A compromise answer?

But, unfortunately, even this can't guarantee success. It may be that you really have more to do than you can possibly manage in the time available. In that case, you could find yourself having to compromise on the answer. Do avoid ever saying 'no' if you possibly can, but you have to accept that there will be times when you have to say 'yes – but...'. The important thing is to try to advance on all fronts – leave everybody with something, rather than some with a complete answer and others with nothing. There are various things you can do to keep to your deadlines.

Suggest sources rather than finding answers

Suggesting sources in which your enquirer can look, rather than finding the answer for them, is an obvious tactic, and enquirers are usually sympathetic if they can see that you're under pressure from other people standing round. But it can be harder to convince them that you are short of time if there's no-one else around, no matter how many jobs you are working on for absent enquirers. And don't expect to get any sympathy if you actually list for the enquirer's edification all the other things you have to do – that's your problem, not theirs. If you do have to resort to suggesting sources, make sure that you explain fully to the enquirer how the source works; show them the different indexes available in a printed source, take them through the various menus or buttons on a database or website. And invite them to return for further advice if the source doesn't work; don't ever give the impression that you're fobbing them off.

Suggest alternative libraries or information services

Suggesting sources doesn't work with telephone or e-mail enquirers. If you can't help them immediately, you could suggest an alternative library or information service that they could try. But again, be as helpful as possible in doing this. Look up the organization's phone number, e-mail address and website in a directory, and tell your enquirer exactly what that library/information service can do that you can't. In some cases, merely giving an e-mail enquirer the web address of a relevant institution may be sufficient in itself, if its site has a good Frequently Asked Questions (FAQs) section. Beware, though, of directing enquirers to services that they are not entitled to use. Some institutions will accept enquiries only from their members or subscribers; others will want to charge.

Ask for thinking time

An alternative tactic when dealing with telephone or email enquirers is to say 'Leave it with me; I'll see what I can do.' This buys you valuable time and leaves the enquirer satisfied that you are taking the enquiry seriously. However, you must take the time straight away to go through the full questioning procedure that we discussed in Chapter 1. You must also agree a deadline with the enquirer – and then meet it.

Offer a quick & dirty answer

Of course, asking for thinking time merely leaves you with yet another deadline to meet. In that case, an alternative tactic is to offer a briefer answer. (This tactic works equally well whether the enquirer is standing in front of you or has got in touch by phone, e-mail or fax.) A quick & dirty answer is usually a briefer one – whatever you can find in a few minutes in readily accessible sources. However there are some occasions when a quick & dirty answer can be a longer one. It might take only a few minutes to do a rough and ready web or database search and hand the results over unchecked for the enquirer to go through in detail in their own time. Whereas, if you had the time yourself, you would take responsibility for going through the results yourself on a word processor, and for removing the less relevant material. (This is all part of adding value, and we'll return to it in Chapter 8.)

Progress reports

Whatever strategies you choose to employ to ensure you meet your deadlines, it's important to keep enquirers informed on how you're getting on. You're likely to do this automatically when the enquirer is standing over you, but you should get into the habit of doing it for absent enquirers too. It's reassuring to the enquirer, and it shows them that you're being open about any difficulties and not trying to pull the wool over their eyes. And, although you'll always hope to succeed in finding the answer, progress reports can also prepare enquirers for disappointment (and put them in a mood for accepting a compromise answer) if your searching is going badly. Making progress reports may seem irksome and time-consuming, but it undoubtedly pays customer relations dividends.

Coming next – what to do if you can't find the answer...

All of this assumes, of course, that you actually have some hope of finding the answer. But what do you do if it's just nowhere to be found? In Chapter 7, we'll think about what to do if your chosen sources fail to come up with the answer at all.

To recap . . .

➤ **Make sure you understand the difference between vital and urgent tasks.**

➤ **Establish a working timetable, grading and prioritizing enquiries according to whether they are easy or hard, quick or slow.**

➤ **Buy time if necessary by supplying sources instead of doing the searching, or suggesting alternative institutions, or asking for thinking time, or offering a quick & dirty answer.**

➤ **Always keep your enquirers informed about progress.**

Chapter 7
Can't find the answer – what now?
What to do if your chosen sources fail

In this chapter you'll find out how to:

➤ **prepare your enquirer for disappointment**
➤ **settle for an alternative answer**
➤ **look for outside help**
➤ **decide whether it's worth buying the information in.**

Some years back, a big motor accessories supplier ran a national advertising campaign under the slogan 'The answer is "yes" – now what's the question?' It was a bit of a cheat because it presumably only meant questions about vehicle parts. But you can't fault the attitude behind it.

We've already looked at the problem of information overload, in Chapter 2. But it has a positive side as well. It means that the likelihood of failing to find an answer to any enquiry is diminishing all the time. More and more information is available online, and technological developments in typesetting and printing mean that more information than ever can also be published cost-effectively in paper form.

Saying 'no' positively

So is there any excuse for failing to find the answer? Sometimes. Your enquirer may decide that the information is just not worth the cost of going online or using a commercial information broker. You may decide that you can't afford to invest the time on a speculative and possibly fruitless attempt to find a website that might be able to help. So, no matter how much technology you surround yourself with, and no matter how well funded your organization is, you might still have to admit defeat.

But this still doesn't mean saying 'no'. It means exercising ingenuity in helping your enquirer to continue travelling hopefully instead of hitting a *cul de sac*. It means thinking positively about what you can still do. Remember the technique you used when your mind went blank in Chapter 3? You said 'I'm sure I can help,' and indeed you still can – although by now not necessarily in the way your enquirer expected.

Preparing your enquirer for disappointment

So it's probably just as well to start lowering your enquirer's expectations as soon as you realize there are going to be difficulties. This is where the progress reports mentioned in Chapter 6 come in. You'll be in a much better position to help your enquirer if they're already aware that you are having problems and are starting to think about what alternative answers would be acceptable.

What you can do to save the situation at this stage will depend on what exactly your enquirer wants the information for. As we discovered in Chapter 2, people rarely want information merely to satisfy idle curiosity – they nearly always have a purpose in asking. This means that you can sometimes accommodate their needs by providing an alternative answer – less specific than the one they asked for, for example, but almost as helpful in enabling them to reach the conclusion they seek or put forward the argument they want to promote. To decide where to look for this, you need to go back to the technique we looked at in Chapter 3, and try to imagine the appearance not of an ideal answer but of an acceptable alternative.

Where else can you go?

If you don't have anything in-house that might provide the answer, then you can always seek outside help. This offers you lots of scope; there are thousands of sources you could consider, and plenty of places you can look to identify them. As we saw in Chapter 6, providing the web address of a relevant institution may offer your enquirer some immediate help. Beyond this, though, seeking outside help usually imposes delays on the answer and, as we again saw in Chapter 6, you frequently don't discover that you're in difficulties until the deadline is looming. So a third possibility is to go online for the information; but this can be expensive, and your enquirer would presumably have to bear the cost.

The really important thing at this stage is to keep your enquirer informed. You have to be realistic about it; you are the bearer of bad news, and your job now is to soften its impact. You need further help from your enquirer on what would be an acceptable way of salvaging the enquiry, so you need to go right back to the kinds of questions and answers that we looked at in Chapter 1 – almost a repeat of the original dialogue, but with a changed agenda.

Of course, you might have anticipated the difficulties, using the easy/hard and quick/slow assessments that we looked at in Chapter 6. And you will of course have decided (as we discussed in Chapter 4) whether to go for the most up to date, most relevant or most appropriate sources first. So you may well be quite clear what your next move must be, without any further reference to your enquirer. But warn them, nevertheless.

Looking for outside help

There are hundreds of possible sources that can lead you to outside help on every conceivable topic, and you will be very unlucky indeed if you can't find anywhere at all to direct your enquirer to. (Have another look at the 25 multi-purpose reference sources at the front of this book; *most* of them can lead you to further sources of help.) Seeking outside help also has the advantage of sticking to the enquirer's agenda, whereas if you suggest a substitute answer, you inevitably shift the agenda to suit you. But going outside does introduce a further delay, and it also means that you can no longer necessarily guarantee the attention and courtesy that you are of course giving your own enquirer. Remember, an unsatisfactory response from a source that you have recommended can rebound on you.

The Westminster Aquarium enquiry is an ideal candidate for referral. Frustrated at your failure to find anything that provides any detail on what must at first have seemed to be a fairly straightforward topic, you do at least know from its name roughly where the building was. You will also be aware – or could speculate – that local history and archive services are a local authority responsibility, and will be able to look up the relevant authority and locate its archives service. This just about the simplest and most straightforward referral you can do.

But it's not the only kind. You might draw a complete blank with the Strong & Moral Britain Association. If it's the kind of organization your enquirer suspects, with neo-Fascist connections, then it might not be particularly forthcoming with information about itself for publication in directories. So that's when you might need to exercise a bit of imagination and think what kinds of alternative sources would be interested in helping. Faced with this situation, there's another hypothetical question you need to ask yourself – and the question is:

Who really needs to know this?

In this case, anti-racist organizations seem the obvious candidates; a quick check of a source like the *Directory of British Associations* would reveal the Institute of Race Relations as one possible candidate, and would tell you whether it had a library or offered an information service.

If you're in the habit of using specialist e-mail discussion lists, then you can of course consider contacting the members of an appropriate list for help. Posting to a discussion list has the advantage of putting the problem before a large number of people; and it only needs one person to have experience of dealing with the same or a similar enquiry in the past for most of your troubles to be over. It may be your only hope in your quest for a song called 'When I would sing under the ocean'; no reference sources are going to reveal it under this title, so you may be completely reliant on a musical colleague with a crossword puzzle mentality making the connection. Don't just take their answer at face value, though, no matter how grateful you are; tactfully double-check the information by looking up 'When I was king of the Beotians' in an encyclopedia of music, a recordings catalogue or perhaps a book of operettas.

If informal discussion lists don't work, you can actually use the web to ask other libraries for help. Ask a Librarian is a splendid cooperative venture involving public library services throughout the UK, whose staff undertake to answer enquiries from the public by e-mail as quickly as possible (www.ask-a-librarian.org.uk). Be very careful not to abuse such a service, though. Remember, enquiry answering is your job and there's no excuse for becoming lazy!

Asking authors or editors

You can use the results of your literature searching for a third type of referral – to the authors of nearly relevant books or articles, or the editors of what seem like appropriate journals. Your hunt for material on the Westminster Aquarium may have led you to a lovely coffee-table book on Victorian pleasure palaces, with just one picture of the Aquarium and a brief caption. So why not try contacting the author? You might find them in one of a number of Who's Who-type publications that cover writers, but sources of this kind are always highly selective in who they include, and are not always particularly up-to-date; so an alternative would be to use the book's publisher as a go-between. Actually this isn't an ideal solution either, because professional authors (as opposed to enthusiasts) are often reluctant to enter into correspondence, and publishers tend to be protective of their authors too. A better alternative might be to scrutinize the bibliography to see if it can lead you to more detailed literature that your enquirer might be able to see in a specialist library, or borrow through the British Library Document Supply Centre.

Contacting authors of articles in specialist journals, or the editors of those journals, can be more fruitful. Driven by their own enthusiasm, they may be more committed to their subject than a jobbing author or commercial book publisher would be. In the Westminster Aquarium enquiry, the classified index to *Willing's Press Guide* ('Consumer: other classifications: historic buildings') reveals the existence of a magazine called *The Victorian*, whose coverage includes 'architecture and social history of the period'. Alternatively, a search in *Directory of British Associations* will reveal the existence of over 20 organizations under 'Architecture: history & preservation'. The website of one of them – the Victorian Society – shows that it is the publisher of *The Victorian*, and that the theme of the July 2001 issue actually was 'Iron and glass: the influence of the Crystal Palace'. Whether or not it mentions the Aquarium remains to be seen – but it's certainly worth following up.

Buying the information in

When you've exhausted all these possibilities, there may be no alternative to buying the information in. You could use directories of information brokers to identify people or institutions that could actually take the enquiry off your hands and do it for you. You'd not only be buying time that you were not able to devote to the enquiry yourself, but probably also some kind of expertise in the subject concerned. If the labour market data in the *New Earnings Survey* turned out to be insufficient for your enquirer about female earnings in Croydon, then you could make use of the expertise of a broker who specialized in locating and supplying statistical data, or who subscribed to services provided by independent pay consultants such as Incomes Data Services (and was licensed to provide them to third parties, of course).

But this can be hugely expensive; you'd be paying every penny of the broker's costs, plus their profit. Costly as it may seem in cash terms, using a commercial online service would almost certainly work out cheaper (assuming, that is, you were a reasonably efficient searcher who worked out their strategy beforehand and got to useful content relatively quickly). An extensive full text news and features retrieval service, such as LexisNexis, or an online library of periodical articles, such as the web version of *British Humanities Index* or the British Library – inside web service may be essential for information on the Strong & Moral Britain Association.

Expensive online?

In real terms, commercial online services are actually becoming cheaper. This is partly because of technological developments, which mean that the prices charged by the existing commercial services have risen by less than the rate of inflation over the years, but it's also because of the available range of pricing packages. If you're likely to be a heavy user of services such as Dialog, DataStar or LexisNexis, then you'd go for a fixed price package involving a substantial payment up-front with effectively unlimited use thereafter.

Alternatively, pricing packages based on the amount of content you retrieved and downloaded would enable you to cherry-pick information as required, perhaps paying for it online with a corporate credit card. Obviously the unit cost of the information you purchased would be higher than if you took out a blanket subscription, but the service wouldn't be costing you a penny when you weren't using it. These are decisions that you will have to take when you're planning the kind of information service most appropriate for your organization. (We'll return to this in Chapter 9.)

Settling for an alternative answer

After you've reviewed all these other options, there's probably nothing else left now but to suggest an alternative answer. Let's have a think about possible substitute answers to a couple of our sample enquiries. There just might not be enough time to undertake a full analysis of all the migration figures for Wales from the Census. But the Office for National Statistics (ONS) website should have led you to *Regional Trends*, an annual digest that includes some population figures for Wales and its surrounding English regions including one short table of net migration figures. Would this be acceptable, given the time available? That would be for your enquirer to decide.

The Westminster Aquarium enquiry is likely to prove particularly frustrating. It will probably take you ages to pull together a pathetic little selection of references. If you've managed a brief entry in an encyclopaedia of London, an illustration from a book of Victorian views, a few sentences gleaned from the indexes of textbooks and a passing reference on a website that you can't really trust, then you'll have done very well indeed. But remember your enquirer told you that they were doing a project – for school or college, one assumes. They need enough material for a 500-word essay, so what can you add?

Bearing in mind your earlier discovery of the Victorian Society, you could suggest broadening the scope of the project to take in some of the context in which the Westminster Aquarium operated. Perhaps it could also cover other popular Victorian entertainment venues in London, or social studies on the growth of working-class wealth and leisure during the nineteenth century. There should be plenty of material on both these topics – indeed, you'll already be in a position to recommend suitable sources, because you've already come across them while actually looking for references to the Aquarium. Your hapless enquirer, whose own deadline will undoubtedly be tight (students only seem to come to a library and information professional for help at the last moment) will probably fall upon you with gratitude. But beware! You've changed the agenda in this enquiry to suit yourself; so be especially sensitive to your enquirer's reaction, to make sure that the suggested change also suits them. Your enquirer will not be impressed if you try to present an alternative answer as a lovely surprise.

Coming next – adding value...

Let's continue on a more positive note. This book is about success, after all. But successful enquiry answering doesn't simply mean handing the answer over with no further comment. It's about making sure that what you provide is the best available, presented to your enquirer in the most helpful way possible. So in the next chapter, we'll look at how to add value to your answers.

To recap . . .

➤ Keep your enquirer informed of difficulties, so that you can both be thinking of acceptable alternative answers.

➤ Look for specialist organizations, authors and bibliographies of nearly relevant literature, and editors of appropriate journals, as possible sources to refer your enquirer to.

➤ Consider using information brokers or commercial online services, bearing in mind cost versus value.

➤ Make sure that any less detailed or broader substitute answer that you provide still addresses your enquirer's needs.

Chapter 8
Success! Now let's add some value
Presenting your answer well is part of the job

In this chapter you'll find out how to:

➤ make sure that you really have answered the question
➤ decide what to leave out of the answer
➤ take time and trouble over presenting what's left – orally, visually.

There can scarcely be a library or information service in the world that believes it is over-funded. More often than not, the staff feel that they're struggling with inadequate resources, and that there simply aren't enough of them to satisfy the demands placed upon the services they provide. That's why the emphasis throughout this book has been on using moderately priced mainstream information sources, and on getting a quart out of a pint pot. Where we have referred to high-priced commercial services, it has always been on the assumption that they are a medium of last resort.

But you can still take pride in the answers you provide. This is partially for your personal satisfaction, but it's also really good customer relations. A service that looks and sounds good inspires customer confidence and wins repeat business; one that doesn't risks losing that confidence, resulting in declining business and possibly even closure. In helping people find the information they want, you haven't been doing something easy, you've been doing something highly skilled. So don't spoil it by presenting the answer sloppily.

Have you really answered it?

But before you present the answer at all, do make sure that you really have answered the question. Go back to your enquiry form, notebook, log or whatever you use in your library or information service, and check the wording carefully. Do this for two reasons – firstly, because you waste your enquirer's time if you find that you've allowed yourself to be unconsciously diverted during the course of your researches. (Remember your exams again – there are no marks for submitting the perfect answer to a question that isn't on the paper.)

Secondly, you need to check because enquirers are quite capable of changing the agenda while you are searching, without bothering to tell you. Remember the problems you encountered in Chapter 1, trying to find out what your enquirers really wanted in the first place? Unfortunately, it doesn't stop there. While you are busy trying to find the answer, your enquirer is still thinking about the question, and probably coming up with all sorts of supplementary information that they'd like as well. Or they may have been pursuing their own researches in parallel to yours, and have already come up with the answer to the question they originally put to you. Annoying as this may be, you have to be tolerant. After all, it's just a job for you, but it might be personally very important for them.

What to leave out

We worried about information overload as early as Chapter 2. But it's now, while you're preparing to present your answer, that it really matters. You may well have found similar information from several different sources. This could be because you were unhappy with the level of detail in the first source you used, and wanted to see whether you could improve on it in another one. Or because you found several articles or news features on the same subject, with huge overlaps between them. Or half a dozen different organizations that you could refer your enquirer to, because you hadn't been able to find the information in-house.

But there's no rule that says you have to provide them all. As the quantity of available information continues to grow, enquirers will be looking to library and information professionals for their expertise not only in finding the right answer but also in judging which is the best *version* of the right answer. There's a rather pretentious saying – 'To govern is to choose'. It implies that making choices is the hardest part of government. It is – it's the hardest part of anything. All information work is about choices – choosing what sources to buy, choosing what index entries to create for them, choosing what to leave out when you write abstracts of them. Why should enquiry work be any different?

Information versus references

Of course, there will be times when you genuinely don't feel well qualified enough to make decisions of this kind – in highly technical subjects such as medicine or law. But even then you can still opt for offering complete texts of only some of the sources, and providing references to the others. That way, you've minimized the amount that your enquirer has to read and, if you've been providing your answer on paper, using photocopies or downloads of key sources (subject to prevailing copyright rules, of course), then you've also been kind to trees.

Whatever you decide to provide, you should always tell your enquirer where the information has come from. It may be tempting to keep these details to yourself, in a misguided attempt to ensure that they remain dependent on you. But resist the temptation. Firstly, it's a very unprofessional practice for one whose job is providing information. Secondly, it's all too easy for an enquirer to go to another library or information service that is prepared to source its information. And thirdly, if your enquirer subsequently comes back for further details, it's extremely embarrassing if you can't remember where the information came from in the first place.

Presenting what's left

So you've found the right answer – perhaps presented in several different ways – and you've decided which version is the best one for your enquirer's purposes. Now all you have to do is hand it over in triumph. So just take a few moments to decide how you're going to do it. After all, you don't want to spoil the climax, do you?

If you're presenting the answer orally, make sure that what you tell your enquirer covers all the points – no less, no more – and warns of any complications or potential pitfalls. If you're responding by phone, remember too that it will probably take a few seconds for the person at the other end to get onto your wavelength. So use those few seconds to introduce yourself, say where you're calling from and remind the enquirer what they asked for. Then check that they've got a pen and paper handy. Then give them the answer. Something like . . .

> Hello, is that Mr Sampson? This is Delilah Milton from the Ghaza Mills Reference Library. You asked me to find Marks & Spencer's current pretax profit, and I have the information for you if you're ready . . . The total operating profit for the year ended 31 March 2002 for the Marks & Spencer group was £629.1 million. The information comes from the company's own website, which you can find at www.marksandspencer.com. They also announced half year profits of £305.8 million in November 2002. The last full year results were announced in May 2002, which suggests that the 2002-2003 figures could be out very soon. Would you like me to let you know when they appear?

Oh and, by the way, if you are on the phone, don't forget to smile.

Enhancing answers on paper

When you're presenting an answer on paper, your scope for adding value is enormously enhanced. Obviously if you're simply handing over an original publication, you'll show the enquirer the relevant passage or entry. So if you're supplying a photocopy for your enquirer to keep, or if you're faxing the information back, mark the crucial sections. Highlight the relevant paragraph with a marker pen. Put asterisks against the most useful entries in a directory. Draw a line down the required column or across the required row of a table of statistics. Put in an arrow head to point out the key component of a diagram. Circle the right place on a map. And, whatever else you do, make sure that the source of your document is clearly cited. Underline it if it's already printed there; write it in if not. And make sure that all the volume, part and page details are included. These are suggestions, of course, not hard and fast rules. But, as a general principle, do whatever you can to lead your enquirer to the information they want as rapidly and clearly as possible.

Many of your enquiries will probably be quick reference affairs, over and done with in a few minutes. But if you regularly carry out extended enquiry work, why not consider handing over the results in a professional presentation folder? For a fee-based enquiry service, quite a lavish pre-printed offering may well be appropriate – it could enhance the perceived value of the information far beyond the cost of the folder itself. But even for more modest offerings, it could well be worth slipping the papers into a clear plastic folder with a smart piece of stationery, bearing your organization's logo, as the top sheet. (And, of course, you'd always include a covering note inviting your enquirer to come back and discuss the outcome if they wished.) The cost of doing something like this is minuscule, the customer relations value immense.

Enhancing answers electronically

With information presented electronically, the number of ways you can enhance it is really limited only by your own imagination. Electronic delivery of answers to enquiries is likely to happen more and more as electronic versions of specialist publications replace print versions, as you take more information from the web, and as growing numbers of your enquirers are able to receive emails.

You can help your enquirer to make sense of a large body of **text** by adding headlines, subheadings and guiding, and by highlighting the key words or phrases in the text in bold or italic. Finding those key words or phrases is easy for you; word processors and web browsers have word search facilities, so it takes only a few seconds to add an enormous amount of value. Alternatively, you could copy key paragraphs out of the original text and paste them in at the head of your answer. This allows your enquirer both to take in the crucial information immediately, and also to read it in its proper context later on. (How do you know what to highlight? You use your mini-thesaurus as a guide.)

You can enhance **figures** in the same way. If you have downloaded some statistical information or other numeric data to a spreadsheet, then it need be the work of only a few minutes to add value by calculating an average for the figures retrieved, or expressing them as percentages for greater clarity, or ranking them. Or you can turn them into a graph, bar or pie chart. Make sure you really understand what you're doing, though. It's all too easy for simple mistakes in spreadsheet creation to render figures seriously misleading, if not downright wrong!

The exponential growth of the web has also enormously increased the value of **images** as sources of information. A picture is worth a thousand words, the cliché goes, and you can exploit this to the limit in your enquiry answering. You can drop images into word-processed documents, or even supply your answer as an audiovisual presentation if you think that's more appropriate. And as with electronic text, you don't necessarily need to show the whole picture; if one detail is particularly important, crop it out of the main image, using image processing software or even simply the image formatting facility on your word processor or audiovisual presentation software.

A word of warning, though: if you are presenting your answers electronically, make sure your virus checking software is up to scratch. Your enquirer will not be pleased if your answer arrives complete with its very own infection.

Copyright, licensing, ethics

And another thing to beware: there are ethical considerations to bear in mind when manipulating text, numbers or images in this way. Be sure that you make it quite clear what you have done with the version of the document that you finally present to your enquirer, so that they are in no doubt as to how it varies from the original. (And, as always, make sure that you cite the source in full in your answer.) Copyright is a vital issue too. Before you engage in activity of this kind, be sure that you understand the terms on which the publication, data or software concerned has been supplied to you. If the licence forbids supply of copies to a third party then, no matter how much you may regret the missed opportunity, you must not do it.

As a general principle, in fact, you should make sure that you understand *all* the photocopying and downloading restrictions under which your library or information service operates before you start any enquiry work. There's plenty of help available if you need it; Facet Publishing (the imprint of CILIP: the Chartered Institute of Library and Information Professionals) produces a range of copyright guides covering circumstances applicable to libraries and information services – check on www.facetpublishing.co.uk for details. As copying in all media becomes easier and easier, publishers understandably become more and more vigilant about infringements. And nothing could be worse for your customer relations than promising something that the rules don't subsequently allow you to deliver.

Coming next – learning from each enquiry...

Your task is nearly over. But before you finally sign the enquiry off, there are some really useful lessons to be learned from it – plus quite possibly new information sources to consider and new services that you could introduce as a result. So in the last chapter of all, we're going to think about what we can learn from each enquiry.

To recap . . .

➤ **Check finally that you really have answered the question; it's all too easy to be diverted, or for enquirers to change their mind.**

➤ **Remember that you don't necessarily have to supply everything you've found; supply the best and refer to the rest.**

➤ **Make sure you cite sources for every piece of information you supply and, if necessary, indicate how it varies from the original.**

➤ **Seize every opportunity to add value; compose your oral answers carefully, highlight key information on paper, enhance downloaded data.**

➤ **Always make sure you operate within copyright and licensing restrictions.**

Chapter 9
Sign-off: what can we learn from this enquiry?
Using completed enquiries to develop your services

> **In this chapter you'll find out how to:**
>
> ➤ assess enquiry performance consistently and objectively
> ➤ review the sources you used with a view to developing new services
> ➤ ensure that you have the right tools for the future.

Sir Winston Churchill famously said at a turning point in the Second World War: 'This is not the end. This is not even the beginning of the end. But it is perhaps the end of the beginning.' And so it is at this stage in your enquiry answering. You've sent the enquirer away satisfied, it's true. But have you done everything you can for your own information service and the facilities it could provide? You've just spent a lot of time working for the benefit of one person or organization – your enquirer. If you left it at that, then you could be missing an opportunity to turn that time spent into a really useful investment.

So take some time to review the completed enquiry. Assess it for its difficulty and the time it took. Look carefully at the sources you used; there are likely to be some new ones, and you need to consider whether or not it might be worth purchasing or subscribing to them. You may possibly have contacted some useful new organizations as well; you'll need to decide how to record them so you can benefit from their expertise again in the future. The enquiry may even have suggested an entirely new service that you could offer as a result, in which case you will have a lot of thinking to do, deciding how best to introduce and manage it.

Completing an enquiry successfully isn't the end; it's the start of the next phase in your enquiry service. So let's look at some of these considerations in more detail . . .

How successful were you?

Just as we said in Chapter 1 that you mustn't accept a vague deadline, so you shouldn't tolerate an imprecise measure of success either. It's all too easy for a complacent colleague to record as 'successful' an enquiry that a more conscientious one might regard as only partially successful. Taken to its extreme, this could result in the more conscientious one ending up with a poorer annual appraisal report than the complacent one, simply because they were more honest and realistic in recording their degree of enquiry answering success.

So instead, you should go for more objective measures of success. Take a look at section 9 of the model enquiry form that we've suggested on page xii. It offers three measures of success – complete, partial or compromise.

'Complete' success

'Complete' success means that you have provided an answer that met the enquirer's needs in every respect; you covered all aspects of the question, and provided an answer that will enable them to make a recommendation, take a decision or take action. In the case of the cash for questions question, for example, this would mean that you had: found some useful news coverage of the cash for questions affair that either mentioned your enquirer's brother or specifically eliminated him; discovered how the Strong & Moral Britain Association was funded and whether or not it was associated with neo-fascist organizations; and been able to provide some authoritative guidelines on what obligations school governors faced regarding declaration of other interests. Anything less than this, and you would probably have to record the degree of success as 'partial'.

'Partial' success

'Partial' success means that you have been able to find some of what the enquirer wants, but not all. You may, for example, have come up with some figures on migration patterns in Wales which show general trends over a period for the whole Principality, but not necessarily the degree of detail that the enquirer would have liked – nothing on specific movements into and out of Glamorgan, for example. In this case, you've certainly provided an answer that will get the enquirer started, but not enough to enable them to finish their task to their satisfaction; so you've probably referred them to somewhere else as well. (We'll deal with recording referrals in a moment.)

'Compromise'

'Compromise' means that you and the enquirer have together agreed on an answer that was not exactly what the enquirer wanted, but which is an acceptable alternative nevertheless. In the Westminster Aquarium query, for example, you may have agreed to supplement the paltry offering you can provide on the Aquarium itself with background on Victorian entertainments, or rival attractions of the period, just to enable the enquirer to complete their project to the satisfaction of the project supervisor. This not an ideal outcome, and you must of course have agreed it with the enquirer. But it's about as close to an admission of failure as you should ever allow your enquiry service to come.

No success?

Note that there is no space for recording that you were unsuccessful; remember the promise you gave when you were starting to think about how you would answer the enquiry back in Chapter 3? 'I'm sure I can help' was what you said – and so you can, even if you and the enquirer eventually had to compromise on what kind of answer would be acceptable. If you ever felt that you had to record an 'unsuccessful' result, then what that would really mean is that the enquiry isn't finished yet. (Note, too, that we haven't talked about referrals yet; we'll come back to those in a moment.)

How long did it take to answer?

Next, you need to record how long the enquiry took to answer. You'll need to consider whether the time it took was pretty much what you would have expected, or whether it took longer. If it did take longer, then was this because it was more difficult than you expected, or just more time-consuming? These are not necessarily the same thing, and it comes back to the easy/quick hard/slow decisions you had to take when you were deciding on the working timetable for prioritizing your enquiries (Chapter 6). For example, hard needn't necessarily mean slow; you may decide that it's going to be so difficult to discover the Strong & Moral Britain Association's neo-fascist connections that you'll speed up the process by using a database rather than a manual search. On the other hand, you might have very easily have found masses of data on migration patterns in Wales, but turning it into a form that was acceptable to the enquirer might have taken an inordinate amount of time.

It is vitally important to know how long enquiries take to answer, because time is money, and if there's a pattern to the difficult and/or lengthy enquiries then that raises implications about the appropriateness and value of the sources you're using. Perhaps you need to invest in something new – and maybe you'll be able to offer some useful new services as a result. (We'll come back to this a little later on.)

Did you meet the deadline?

Then you need to know whether you met the enquirer's deadline. There are only two possible answers to this – yes or no. Nothing else will do, and if you're recording a lot of 'No's in this box then, again, you need to do some serious thinking about why, and what you need to do to improve your 'Yes' score. If you had to negotiate more time (You didn't just present a late answer without warning the enquirer that that was going to happen, did you?), then you need to record your reasons – not just to get you off the hook but so you can decide what service improvements are needed to try to prevent it happening again. It may well be that the enquiry took a long time because you just didn't know what would be the best sources to get you started. Well, now you do. So record them, and make use of what you have learned the next time a similar enquiry comes up. (We'll come back to this too in a moment.)

Did you have to refer the enquiry elsewhere?

If you recorded partial success or a compromise outcome, then that may well mean that you also referred the enquiry to another organization. This should trigger a whole range of questions about how your service might be able to change and develop as a result. If it's an organization that you have never used before then, firstly, how did you discover it? If it was in a directory, then does that mean that that directory is actually more useful than you might previously have imagined? Have you checked the new organization's web site to find out what else it can offer? Is that site worth bookmarking for future reference? And, if so, where is the best place to put it amongst your list of favourites?

And what about the organization itself? When you contacted it (You did contact it, didn't you? You didn't just leave the enquirer to make a cold call?), were the staff both helpful and useful (not necessarily the same thing)? If they were both helpful and useful, did they help out of goodwill? Or does the organization have an agenda to pursue? If the former, then you should certainly be grateful, but shouldn't necessarily rely on that goodwill persisting if you keep going back to the same organization time and time again. At some point, you'll need to decide what kind of long term relationship you need to have with it (see below.) If it has an agenda, then that's fine just as long as you're clear what that agenda is. If, for example, you decided to contact the Commission for Racial Equality to find out more about the Strong & Moral Britain Association, then you can be quite clear that the CRE would be strongly opposed to the Association's activities and could evaluate its response to your enquiry accordingly. But things aren't always necessarily that clear cut. If you contact an industry or trade organization, for example, then you'll need to know whether it's on the producer or consumer side of the fence, or whether it represents employers or employees.

Melodramatic as it may seem, you'll also need to know whether the organizations you contact are discreet. If an enquirer approaches an organization on your advice, and subsequently finds themselves bombarded with unsolicited communications from it, then they're likely to be upset with you. And if your approach to the organization or – even worse – your enquirer's approach becomes public without your or their consent, then you're in even bigger trouble. You may of course have redress against the organization under data protection rules, but by that time the damage will have been done. So the moral is: check immediately that the organization handles all enquiries in confidence.

Assuming that your referral organization has passed all these tests, then you'll finally need to consider your long-term relationship with it. It may be a trade association or professional body that offers a charged-for enquiry or advice service, which you might consider subscribing to.

This is a big decision, of course, with implications for your budget. So it's not to be undertaken lightly. But you can't undertake it at all unless you have recorded the enquiry properly in the first place.

Did you discover any useful new sources?

It's not at all unusual to discover that a source you already have in stock but have never really had the time to get to know properly turns out to be ideal for a particular kind of enquiry that has always foxed you in the past. Multi-purpose sources such as *Whitaker's Almanac* are crammed with useful snippets of information that you wouldn't necessarily expect to find there and, ironically, your colleagues in smaller, less well resourced services are far more likely to know about them because they will have got into the habit of making the most of the limited range of sources at their disposal.

So when you do discover a useful new source – whether print or electronic – do make sure you have procedures in place for recording it properly. A good technique is your own organization's customized Frequently Asked Questions (FAQs) facility. The form it takes will depend on the nature of the searching aids you have already chosen to develop for your service. It could possibly just be a regularly updated list on paper that you keep at the enquiry desk, but this seems a less and less satisfactory solution when there are so many more effective and flexible methods you could employ. So consider instead creating an in-house database – whether using a database package or simply a word processor. Instantly updatable at any time, it will almost certainly enable you to create automatic links to any websites or e-mail addresses you include in it.

Put it on your network drive, if you can, so everybody in the organization can have access to it. (It would be wise to make it a read-only file, so that only you can make changes to it after due consideration of the value of any new entry you want to add, and so you can be sure that the indexing of your FAQs facility remains up to standard.) If your organization has an intranet, then that would seem the obvious place to include an FAQs page based on your stock and services. It means that you can also include live links to internal sources of information or expertise within your organization, creating the beginnings of a knowledge management system in which your library or information service has seized the initiative.

Does this mean that you are giving away trade secrets, and putting your service at risk as a result? No – quite the reverse. It means that you're constantly drawing your users' attention to your services, and demonstrating your expertise at the same time.

When you discover a new source that you don't actually have, then of course you have to consider whether it's worth purchasing or subscribing to. If you decide that it is, then you should consider which medium would be most appropriate for you (see Chapter 4 for details) and you'll also need to examine any copyright or licensing requirements, to ensure that you are entitled to exploit it in the way you want (Chapter 8). If, for example, you intend to network the new source direct to your users throughout the organization, then there are likely to be cost implications, because licence fees often vary depending on how many desks you intend to network the service to.

Whether you have access to a corporate intranet and can provide a networked current awareness service, or whether you have to rely simply on a printed newsletter or even notices by the enquiry desk, you should always have procedures in place for telling both your colleagues and your users about new services that you can offer as a result of new sources acquired. And remember, too, that it should be that way round; the services should come first, not the sources. Your enquirers aren't interested in sources, but in outcomes.

Looking to the future

How can you be sure, though, that you're offering services that your users really need, and haven't just got carried away with excitement at a newly discovered source? This is the time to ask yourself – and keep asking yourself – whether the services you are offering really meet your organization's needs. If you are providing a general reference service in a public library, or supporting students and academics in an educational library, then you probably have to be ready for just about anything your enquirers might throw at you, and try to remain equipped with a wide range of sources appropriate for the purpose. If, on the other hand, you're providing a service for one organization, then you have lots of scope for tailoring that service to your organization's specific needs.

How might you set about this? Firstly, you should get into the habit of reading your organization's corporate literature – its annual report, promotional publications and special reports. Make sure, too, that you know its website and intranet inside out. Try talking to the senior people, and asking them to think of instances when they've had difficulty finding vital pieces of information. (If it's a large organization, and you find it hard to get access to the top people, ask for introductions from your own head of department – or from someone who interviewed you for your job.) All of this should give you a shopping list of your organization's actual and implicit information requirements. Only then can you start to decide what new information sources you might need.

You'll probably want to know first of all what is going on in your organization's special field at the moment. For this you'll need subscriptions to the trade press, relevant professional journals and online newsletters, and discussion lists. You'll also need the main directories relevant to your organization's specialism. (Some of the 25 multi-purpose reference sources on page xv of this book will help you to identify the publications, information services and websites you need.)

Exploiting your sources actively

Once you've started acquiring the tools for the job, then you should exploit them actively. Scan the trade magazines. If you can use them to provide a current awareness service, excellent! But even if you haven't got the time to do that, becoming familiar with the current issues of concern and the terminology will help you deal with the panic that we considered in Chapter 3 when the enquiries come in.

You should also use the trade magazines to discover newly published reports in your field (using the rapid reading techniques we discussed in Chapter 5); you'll probably be surprised at how many news items are based on new publications, and this can be a very valuable way of building up your current stock quickly. Use the book reviews section of professional journals too, to build up your core stocks of textbooks. Use the directories to follow up contacts that might be able to help you with future enquiries. All this should help you with your immediate information needs, but you'll also need to be ready to deal with requests for older material as well. You'll want to investigate online libraries of journal articles such as the British Library – inside web service, Emerald or Ingenta. For even older and more obscure material, you may well need to use the British Library Document Supply Service too – see www.bl.uk/services/document.html for details.

This can all take time that you may feel you can ill afford when there are immediate pressing enquiries to be answered. But do try to make time to investigate new sources and to make sure you are fully exploiting the ones you already have. It will pay enormous dividends, and will mean that you will be able to provide an even better enquiry service in the future.

Your goal: successful enquiry answering – every time

So that's it! With a little care and common sense – plus a lively and imaginative approach – you can make enquiry answering one of the most satisfying and fulfilling work activities there is. The explosion of available information, the technological developments that can help you retrieve and enhance it, and the enormously increased public awareness of the value of information – all combine to make the prospects for library and information professionals more exciting than ever before. So the only thing that remains to be done now is to wish you success with your enquiry answering – every time.

To recap . . .

➤ **Try to quantify the degree of success achieved in each enquiry; don't settle for a subjective measurement.**

➤ **If you had difficulty in meeting the enquirer's deadline, think about sources or services that could help you answer a similar enquiry faster next time.**

➤ **If you referred the enquiry to another organization, consider how helpful it was, and whether you could use it again.**

➤ **Make sure you integrate any new sources discovered during the enquiry with your existing ones.**

➤ **Make sure your service always remains relevant to your organization's needs.**

Chapter 10
Guide to key reference sources
Full details of key sources mentioned in the book, with annotations

Full details of all the twenty-five multi-purpose reference sources listed on page xv, and their international equivalents, appear here – plus a few additional ones that are useful for getting started on a wide range of enquiries. Most of these sources started as printed publications, but many are now also available electronically – via the web or on CD-ROM – and some are web-only. This situation is changing all the time as publishers adapt their titles and content to reflect the requirements and capabilities of electronic media, so for this reason I haven't given ISBNs or ISSNs. The information for this bibliography has been taken from publishers' websites. When investigating any of these sources, I strongly recommend that you visit the publisher's website too, to make sure that you have access to the most up-to-date information available.

Abstracts in New Technologies and Engineering
Subject index (with brief abstracts from 1993) to articles in UK and US science and technology journals. Available in print and online.
Companion sources: *British Humanities Index, Applied Social Sciences Index and Abstracts, Sociological Abstracts*.
Comparable sources: *Applied Science & Technology Index and Abstracts/full text, General Science Abstracts/full text*.
CSA, 3rd Floor, Farrington House, Wood Street, East Grinstead, West Sussex RH19 1UZ. Tel: 01342 310480. Fax: 01342 310487. E-mail: sales@csa.com. Web: www.csa.com.

Annual Abstract of Statistics
Comprehensive collection of statistics on all subjects, usually abstracted from more detailed government statistical publications.

Also available online at www.statistics.gov.uk.
Companion sources: *Regional Trends, Social Trends*.
Complementary sources: *Eurostat Yearbook, United Nations Statistical Yearbook*.
Office for National Statistics. Available through TSO, PO Box 29, St Crispin's, Duke Street, Norwich NR3 1GN. Tel: 0870 600 5522. Fax: 0870 600 5533. E-mail: customer.services@tso.co.uk. Web: www.tso.co.uk.

Annual Register

Provides details of the year's events on a country-by-country basis, plus a political, social and economic overview of each country.
Comparable sources: *Europa World Year Book* (much bigger), *Statesman's Yearbook*.
Keesing's Worldwide, 28a Hills Road, Cambridge CB2 1LA. Tel: 01223 508050. Fax: 01223 508049. E-mail: info@keesings.com. Web: www.keesings.com.

Applied Science & Technology Index and Abstracts/full text

Subject index, with abstracts and latterly full text, to articles in English language science and technology journals published worldwide. Available in print, on CD-ROM and online.
Companion sources: *General Science Abstracts/full text, Humanities Index/Abstracts/full text, Social Sciences Index/Abstracts/full text, Wilson OmniFile Full Text Mega Edition*.
Comparable source: *Abstracts in New Technologies and Engineering*.
H W Wilson Co, 950 University Avenue, Bronx, New York 10452. Tel: 00 1 718 588 8400. Fax: 00 1 718 590 1617. E-mail: custserv@hwwilson.com.
UK & European agent: Thompson Henry Ltd, London Road, Sunningdale, Berks SL5 0EP. Tel: 01344 624615. Fax: 01344 626120. E-mail: thl@thompsonhenry.co.uk. Web: www.hwwilson.com.

Applied Social Sciences Index and Abstracts

Subject index, with abstracts, to articles mostly in United Kingdom social science journals. Available in print and online.

95

Companion sources: *Abstracts in New Technologies and Engineering, British Humanities Index, Sociological Abstracts*.
Comparable source: *Social Sciences Index/Abstracts/full text*.
CSA, 3rd Floor, Farrington House, Wood Street, East Grinstead, West Sussex RH19 1UZ. Tel: 01342 310480. Fax: 01342 310487. E-mail: sales@csa.com. Web: www.csa.com.

Aslib Directory of Information Sources in the United Kingdom
Gives details of services available from special libraries and information units, including terms and conditions for access.
Aslib Books & Directories, Aslib/Europa, 11 New Fetter Lane, London EC4P 4EE. Tel: 020 7822 4341. Fax: 020 7822 4329. E-mail: info.europa@tandf.co.uk. Web: www.europapublications.co.uk.

BBC News Online
Comprehensive general news service updated throughout the day with a fully searchable archive.
Comparable service: *Keesing's Record of World Events*.
Web: http://news.bbc.co.uk.

Benn's Media
Gives full publication details of newspapers and journals by subject.
Competitor: *Willing's Press Guide*.
Comparable source: *Ulrich's Periodicals Directory*.
Annual. 3 vols: United Kingdom, Europe, World.
CMP Information Ltd, Riverbank House, Angel Lane, Tonbridge, Kent TN9 1SE. Tel: 01732 362666. Fax: 01732 367301. E-mail: enquiries@cmpinformation.com. Web: www.cmpdata.com.

British Humanities Index
Subject index (with abstracts from 1991) to articles in British and other English language humanities journals. Available in print and online.
Companion sources: *Abstracts in New Technologies and Engineering, Applied Social Sciences Index and Abstracts, Sociological Abstracts*.
Comparable source: *Humanities Index/Abstracts/full text*.

CSA, 3rd Floor, Farrington House, Wood Street, East Grinstead, West Sussex RH19 1UZ. Tel: 01342 310480. Fax: 01342 310487. E-mail: sales@csa.com. Web: www.csa.com.

British Library – inside web

Subscription-based online service that allows you to search for thousands of journal articles and conference papers by title and order them online.

Comparable services: Emerald, Ingenta, *Wilson OmniFile Full Text Mega Edition*.

Web: www.bl.uk/services/current/inside.html.

British Library public catalogue

Includes entries for all the items available from the British Library, either for reference, loan or supply as photocopies. Also provides links to other leading UK and overseas library catalogues.

Comparable services: *British National Bibliography*, *Global Books in Print*, Whitaker LibWeb.

Web: www.bl.uk/catalogues/blpc.html.

British National Bibliography

Gives details of all books and pamphlets placed on legal deposit in the British Library, classified by subject. Available in print and on CD-ROM.

Comparable services: British Library public catalogue, *Global Books in Print*, Whitaker LibWeb.

British Library, National Bibliographic Service, Boston Spa, Wetherby, West Yorkshire LS23 7BQ. Tel: 01937 546585. Fax: 01937 546586. E-mail: nbs-info@bl.uk. Web: www.bl.uk.

Centres, Bureaux & Research Institutes

Gives details of centres of expertise in a wide range of fields.

Companion sources: *Councils, Committees & Boards, Current British Directories, Directory of British Associations & Associations in Ireland, Directory of European Industrial & Trade Associations, Directory of European Professional & Learned Societies, Pan-European Associations*.

CBD Research Ltd, 15 Wickham Road, Beckenham, Kent BR3 2JS. Tel: 020 8650 7745. Fax: 020 8650 0768. E-mail: cbd@cbdresearch.com. Web: www.cbdresearch.com.

Copyright guides

Series of short guides to copyright law as it applies to various different kinds of library. (Various titles & editions).

Companion sources: *A guide to finding quality information on the internet: selection and evaluation strategies, Know it all, find it fast: an A-Z source guide for the enquiry desk, The library and information professional's guide to the internet, The public librarian's guide to the internet, Walford's guide to reference material.*

Facet Publishing, 7 Ridgmount Street, London WC1E 7AE. Tel: 020 7255 0594. Fax: 020 7255 0591. E-mail: info@facetpublishing.co.uk. Web: www.facetpublishing.co.uk.

Councils, Committees & Boards

Gives details of official and public bodies and quangos in the United Kingdom.

Current British Directories

Describes contents of directories and reference works published in the UK.

Comparable source: *Ulrich's Periodicals Directory.*

Companion sources to both: *Centres, Bureaux & Research Institutes, Directory of British Associations & Associations in Ireland, Directory of European Industrial & Trade Associations, Directory of European Professional & Learned Societies, Pan-European Associations.*

CBD Research Ltd, 15 Wickham Road, Beckenham, Kent BR3 2JS. Tel: 020 8650 7745. Fax: 020 8650 0768. E-mail: bd@cbdresearch.com. Web: www.cbdresearch.com.

Dialog
Dialog DataStar
Dialog Profound

Multipurpose online information services permitting sophisticated searching of thousands of sources with global coverage on all subjects.

Comparable services: Factiva, LexisNexis.
Web: www.dialog.com.

Directory of British Associations & Associations in Ireland
Directory of European Industrial & Trade Associations
Directory of European Professional & Learned Societies
Uniform series giving details of associations, societies and other organizations throughout the UK and Europe respectively.
Companion sources: *Centres, Bureaux & Research Institutes, Councils, Committees & Boards, Current British Directories, Pan-European Associations.*
Comparable sources: *Encyclopaedia of Associations: International Organizations, Europa Directory of International Organizations, World Directory of Trade and Business Associations, Yearbook of International Organizations.*
CBD Research Ltd, 15 Wickham Road, Beckenham, Kent BR3 2JS.
Tel: 020 8650 7745. Fax: 020 8650 0768. E-mail:
cbd@cbdresearch.com. Web: www.cbdresearch.com.

Emerald
Provides searchable abstracts and full text of management, technology and library & information journal articles.
Comparable services British Library – Inside web, Ingenta, *Wilson OmniFile Full Text Mega Edition.*
Web: www.emeraldinsight.com.

Encyclopaedia of Associations: International Organizations
Gives details of professional and trade associations, societies and institutions in the United States and internationally.
Competitors: *Europa Directory of International Organizations, Yearbook of International Organizations.*
Comparable sources: *Pan-European Associations, World Directory of Trade & Business Associations.*
Thomson Learning (EMEA), High Holborn House, 50-51 Bedford Row, London WC1R 4LR. Tel: 020 7607 2500. Fax: 020 7067 2600.
E-mail: galeord@gale.com. Web: www.gale.com.

Europa Directory of International Organisations
Gives details of international and world regional organizations.
Competitors: *Encyclopaedia of Associations: International Organizations, Yearbook of International Organizations*
Comparable sources: *Pan-European Associations, World Directory of Trade and Business Associations*.

Europa World Yearbook
Describes the political, social and economic life of each country of the world, with details of main institutions.
Comparable sources (but much shorter): *Annual Register, Statesman's Yearbook*.
Complementary source: *UK... the Official Yearbook of the United Kingdom of Great Britain and Northern Ireland*.
Companion source to both: *World of Learning*.
Europa Publications, 11 New Fetter Lane, London EC4P 4EE. Tel: 020 7822 4300. Fax: 020 7822 4329. E-mail: info.europa@tandf.co.uk. Web: www.europapublications.co.uk.

Eurostat Yearbook
Comprehensive collection of statistics on all subjects, comparing European Union member states and usually abstracted from more detailed Eurostat publications.
Complementary sources: *Annual Abstract of Statistics, United Nations Statistical Yearbook*.
Office for National Statistics. Available through TSO (for Eurostat), PO Box 29, St Crispin's, Duke Street, Norwich NR3 1GN. Tel: 0870 600 5522. Fax: 0870 600 5533. E-mail: customer.services@tso.co.uk. (Equivalent agents operate in other European Union member states as well; see Eurostat website for details.) Web: www.tso.co.uk. Eurostat web: http://europa.eu.int/comm/eurostat.

Factiva
Online information service provided by Reuters (UK) and Dow Jones (US) permitting sophisticated searching of business information sources of all kinds.
Comparable services: DataStar, Dialog, LexisNexis.
Web: www.factiva.com.

General Science Abstracts/full text

Subject index, with abstracts and some full text, to articles in English language science journals published worldwide. Available in print, on CD-ROM and online.

Companion sources: *Applied Science & Technology Index and Abstracts/full text, Humanities Index/Abstracts/full text, Social Sciences Index/Abstracts/full text, Wilson OmniFile Full Text Mega Edition.*

Comparable source: *Abstracts in New Technologies and Engineering.*

H W Wilson Co, 950 University Avenue, Bronx, New York 10452. Tel: 00 1 718 588 8400. Fax: 00 1 718 590 1617. E-mail: custserv@hwwilson.com.

UK & European agent: Thompson Henry Ltd, London Road, Sunningdale, Berks SL5 0EP. Tel: 01344 624615. Fax: 01344 626120. E-mail: thl@thompsonhenry.co.uk. Web: www.hwwilson.com.

Global Books in Print

Gives bibliographic details of currently available English language books worldwide. Available on CD-ROM and online as www.globalbooksinprint.com.

Comparable services: British Library public catalogue, *British National Bibliography*, Whitaker LibWeb.

Bowker, Windsor Court, East Grinstead House, East Grinstead, West Sussex RH19 1XA. Tel: 01342 336179. Fax: 01342 336198. E-mail: customer.services@bowker.co.uk. Web: www.bowker.co.uk.

A guide to finding quality information on the internet: selection and evaluation strategies

Suggests strategies for locating, selecting and evaluating the quality information on the net. By Alison Cooke.

Companion sources: *Know it all, find it fast: an A-Z source guide for the enquiry desk, The library and information professional's guide to the internet, The public librarian's guide to the internet, Walford's guide to reference material*, Copyright guides.

Facet Publishing, 7 Ridgmount Street, London WC1E 7AE. Tel: 020 7255 0594. Fax: 020 7255 0591. E-mail: info@facetpublishing.co.uk. Web: www.facetpublishing.co.uk.

Hollis UK Press & Public Relations Annual
Hollis Europe: the Directory of European Public Relations & PR Networks
Companion volumes giving details of public relations departments and press offices of a very large number of organizations. Also available online.
Hollis Directories Ltd, Harlequin House, 7 High Street, Teddington, Middlesex TW11 8EL. Tel: 020 8977 7711. Fax: 020 8977 1133. E-mail: orders@hollis-pr.co.uk. Web: www.hollis-pr.com.

Humanities Index/Abstracts/full text
Subject index, latterly with abstracts and full text, to articles in English language humanities journals published worldwide. Available in print, on CD-ROM and online.
Companion sources: *Applied Science & Technology Index and Abstracts/full text, General Science Abstracts/full text, Social Sciences Index/Abstracts/full text, Wilson OmniFile Full Text Mega Edition.*
Comparable source: *British Humanities Index.*
H W Wilson Co, 950 University Avenue, Bronx, New York 10452. Tel: 00 1 718 588 8400. Fax: 00 1 718 590 1617. E-mail: custserv@hwwilson.com.
UK & European agent: Thompson Henry Ltd, London Road, Sunningdale, Berks SL5 0EP. Tel: 01344 624615. Fax: 01344 626120. E-mail: thl@thompsonhenry.co.uk. Web: www.hwwilson.com.

Ingenta
Provides full text of articles from a large number of academic and professional journals.
Comparable services: British Library – inside web, Emerald, Wilson omnifile full text mega edition.
Web: www.ingenta.com.

Keesing's Record of World Events
Provides summaries of news from around the world, with regularly updated subject indexes. Available in print, on CD-ROM and online.
Comparable service: BBC News online.

Keesing's Worldwide, 28a Hills Road, Cambridge CB2 1LA. Tel: 01223 508050. Fax: 01223 508049. E-mail: info@keesings.com. Web: www.keesings.com.

Know it all, find it fast: an A-Z source guide for the enquiry desk
Arranged by subject, suggests a wide range of sources, both printed and electronic, that will help answer some of the commonest enquiries. By Bob Duckett, Peter Walker and Christinea Donnelly. Companion sources: *A guide to finding quality information on the internet: selection and evaluation strategies, The library and information professional's guide to the internet, The public librarian's guide to the internet, Walford's guide to reference material,* Copyright guides.
Facet Publishing, 7 Ridgmount Street, London WC1E 7AE. Tel: 020 7255 0594. Fax: 020 7255 0591. E-mail: info@facetpublishing.co.uk. Web: www.facetpublishing.co.uk.

LexisNexis
Multipurpose online information service permitting sophisticated searching of newspaper and journal articles and legal information sources; still significant US focus but other coverage improving. Comparable services DataStar, Dialog and Factiva.
Web: www.lexisnexis.com.

The library and information professional's guide to the internet
Provides comprehensive guidance on how to use the full range of internet-based services and facilities. By Alan Poulter, Debra Hiom and Gwyneth Tseng.
Companion sources: *A guide to finding quality information on the internet: selection and evaluation strategies, Know it all, find it fast: an A-Z source guide for the enquiry desk, The public librarian's guide to the internet, Walford's guide to reference material,* Copyright guides.
Facet Publishing, 7 Ridgmount Street, London WC1E 7AE. Tel: 020 7255 0594. Fax: 020 7255 0591. E-mail: info@facetpublishing.co.uk. Web: www.facetpublishing.co.uk.

103

National Statistics

Provides large number of UK statistics online, plus guidance on the full range of official statistics available elsewhere as well.
Comparable service: United Nations Statistics Division.
Web: www.statistics.gov.uk.

Pan-European Associations

Gives details of Europe-wide professional and trade associations, societies and institutions.
Companion sources: *Centres, Bureaux & Research Institutes, Councils, Committees & Boards, Current British Directories, Directory of British Associations, Directory of European Industrial & Trade Associations, Directory of European Professional & Learned Societies.*
Comparable sources: *Encyclopaedia of Associations: International Organizations, World Directory of Trade and Business Associations, Yearbook of International Organizations.*
CBD Research Ltd, 15 Wickham Road, Beckenham, Kent BR3 2JS.
Tel: 020 8650 7745. Fax: 020 8650 0768. E-mail:
cbd@cbdresearch.com. Web: www.cbdresearch.com.

The public librarian's guide to the internet

Covers the basics of the internet and includes advice on the best websites on specific subjects. Useful for far more than just public librarians! By Sally Criddle, Alison McNab, Sarah Ormes, Ian Winship.
Companion sources: *A guide to finding quality information on the internet: selection and evaluation strategies, Know it all, find it fast: an A-Z source guide for the enquiry desk, The library and information professional's guide to the internet, Walford's guide to reference material,* Copyright guides.
Facet Publishing, 7 Ridgmount Street, London WC1E 7AE. Tel: 020 7255 0594. Fax: 020 7255 0591. E-mail: info@facetpublishing.co.uk.
Web: www.facetpublishing.co.uk.

Regional Trends

Comprehensive collection of statistics on all subjects, comparing

each of the United Kingdom standard regions. Also available online at www.statistics.gov.uk.
Companion sources: *Annual Abstract of Statistics, Social Trends*.
Office for National Statistics. Available through TSO, PO Box 29, St Crispin's, Duke Street, Norwich NR3 1GN. Tel: 0870 600 5522. Fax: 0870 600 5533. E-mail: customer.services@tso.co.uk. Web: www.tso.co.uk.

Social Sciences Index/Abstracts/full text

Subject index, latterly with abstracts and full text, to articles in English language social science journals published worldwide. Available in print, on CD-ROM and online.
Companion sources: *Applied Science & Technology Index and Abstracts/full text, General Science Abstracts, Humanities Index/Abstracts/full text, Wilson OmniFile Full Text Mega Edition*.
Comparable sources: *Applied Social Sciences Index and Abstracts, Sociological Abstracts*.
H W Wilson Co, 950 University Avenue, Bronx, New York 10452. Tel: 00 1 718 588 8400. Fax: 00 1 718 590 1617. E-mail: custserv@hwwilson.com.
UK & European agent: Thompson Henry Ltd, London Road, Sunningdale, Berks SL5 0EP. Tel: 01344 624615. Fax: 01344 626120. E-mail: thl@thompsonhenry.co.uk. Web: www.hwwilson.com.

Social Trends

Selection of statistics on a wide range of British social issues, taken from more detailed government statistical publications. Also available online at www.statistics.gov.uk.
Companion sources: *Annual Abstract of Statistics, Regional Trends*.
Complementary source: *World Marketing Data and Statistics*.
Office for National Statistics. Available through TSO, PO Box 29, St Crispin's, Duke Street, Norwich NR3 1GN. Tel: 0870 600 5522. Fax: 0870 600 5533. E-mail: customer.services@tso.co.uk. Web: www.tso.co.uk.

Sociological Abstracts
Subject index, with abstracts, to articles, books, chapters and conference papers internationally on the social and behavioural sciences. Available in print and online.
Companion sources: *Abstracts in New Technologies and Engineering, Applied Social Sciences Index and Abstracts, British Humanities Index.*
Comparable source: *Social Sciences Index/Abstracts/full text.*
CSA, 3rd Floor, Farrington House, Wood Street, East Grinstead, West Sussex RH19 1UZ. Tel: 01342 310480. Fax: 01342 310487. E-mail: sales@csa.com. Web: www.csa.com.

Sources of Non-Official UK Statistics
Gives details of non-governmental statistical sources, mostly relating to business and industry. By David Mort.
Complementary source: *World Directory of Non-Official Statistical Sources.*
Gower Publishing Ltd, Gower House, Croft Road, Aldershot, Hants GU11 3HR. Tel: 01252 331551. Fax: 01252 344405. E-mail: info@gowerpub.com. Web: www.gowerpub.com.

Statesman's Yearbook
Describes the political, social and economic life of each country of the world, with details of main institutions.
Comparable sources: *Annual Register, Europa World Yearbook* (much bigger).
Complementary source: *UK... the Official Yearbook of the United Kingdom of Great Britain and Northern Ireland.*
Palgrave Macmillan Ltd, Houndmills, Basingstoke, Hampshire, RG21 6XS. Tel: Tel: 01256 329242. Fax: 01256 328339. E-mail: bookenquiries@palgrave.com. Web: www.palgrave.com.

UK... the Official Yearbook of the United Kingdom of Great Britain and Northern Ireland
Describes British political, social and economic life and gives details of principal United Kingdom institutions.
Complementary sources: *Europa World Yearbook, Statesman's Yearbook.*

106

Office for National Statistics. Available through TSO, PO Box 29, St Crispin's, Duke Street, Norwich NR3 1GN. Tel: 0870 600 5522. Fax: 0870 600 5533. E-mail: customer.services@tso.co.uk. Web: www.tso.co.uk.

Ulrich's Periodicals Directory

Gives details of major journals, directories and yearbooks published worldwide by subject. Also available on disc and online at www.ulrichsweb.com.

Comparable sources: *Benn's Media, Current British Directories, Willing's Press Guide.*

Bowker, Windsor Court, East Grinstead House, East Grinstead, West Sussex RH19 1XA. Tel: 01342 336179. Fax: 01342 336198. E-mail: customer.services@bowker.co.uk. Web: www.bowker.co.uk.

United Nations Statistics Division

Provides online a range of international comparative statistical data on a wide variety of topics.

Comparable service: National Statistics.

Web: http://unstats.un.org/ unsd.

United Nations Statistical Yearbook

Comprehensive collection of statistics on all subjects, comparing most countries of the world. Many statistics also available online from the United Nations Statistics Division at http://unstats.un.org/unsd.

Complementary sources: *Annual Abstract of Statistics, Eurostat Yearbook.*

United National Department of Economic & Social Affairs Statistics Division. TSO, PO Box 29, St Crispin's, Duke Street, Norwich NR3 1GN. Tel: 0870 600 5522. Fax: 0870 600 5533. E-mail: customer.services@tso.co.uk. Web: www.tso.co.uk.

Walford's guide to reference material

Describes mostly UK reference sources on all subjects, including sourcebooks, directories & yearbooks, journals, statistics and selected textbooks. 3 vols: Science & technology; Social & historical sciences; Generalia, language, literature, arts.

Companion sources: *A guide to finding quality information on the internet: selection and evaluation strategies, Know it all, find it fast: an A-Z source guide for the enquiry desk, The library and information professional's guide to the internet, The public librarian's guide to the internet,* Copyright guides.

Facet Publishing, 7 Ridgmount Street, London WC1E 7AE. Tel: 020 7255 0594. Fax: 020 7255 0591. E-mail: info@facetpublishing.co.uk. Web: www.facetpublishing.co.uk.

Whitaker LibWeb

Online service giving details of current and out-of-print UK books, and US titles as well.

Comparable services: British Library public catalogue, *British National Bibliography, Global Books in Print.*

Web: www.whitaker.co.uk/libweb1.htm.

Whitaker's Almanac

Comprehensive repository of brief information on all subjects, from a British point of view; a good starting point for information for which there is no obvious specialist source.

A&C Black, 37 Soho Square, London W1D 3QZ. Tel: 020 7758 0200. E-mail: whitakers@acblack.com. Web: www.acblack.com.

Willing's Press Guide

Gives full publication details of newspapers and journals by subject. 3 vols: UK, Europe & World. Also available online.

Competitor: *Benn's Media.*

Comparable source: *Ulrich's Periodicals Directory.*

Waymaker Ltd, Chess House, 34 Germain Street, Chesham, Bucks HP5 1SJ. Tel: 0870 7360010. Fax: 01342 335612. E-mail: willings@waymaker.co.uk. Web: www.willingspress.com.

Wilson OmniFile Full Text Mega Edition

Includes subject index entries and, where available, abstracts and full text drawn from the full range of H W Wilson services, including *General Science Abstracts/full text, Humanities Index/Abstracts/full text* and *Social Sciences Index/Abstracts/full text*. Available online only. Comparable services: British Library – inside web, Emerald, Ingenta.

H W Wilson Co, 950 University Avenue, Bronx, New York 10452. Tel: 00 1 718 588 8400. Fax: 00 1 718 590 1617. E-mail: custserv@hwwilson.com.

UK & European agent: Thompson Henry Ltd, London Road, Sunningdale, Berks SL5 0EP. Tel: 01344 624615. Fax: 01344 626120. E-mail: thl@thompsonhenry.co.uk. Web: www.hwwilson.com.

World Directory of Non-Official Statistical Sources

Gives references to statistics from non-government sources worldwide.

Complementary source: *Sources of Non-Official UK Statistics.*

World Directory of Trade and Business Associations

Gives details of trade and business associations worldwide.

Comparable sources: *Directory of European Industrial & Trade Associations, Encyclopaedia of Associations: International Organizations, Europa Directory of International Organizations, Pan-European Associations, Yearbook of International Organizations.*

World Marketing Data and Statistics

Gives demographic, socio-economic and financial facts and figures for countries worldwide. Also available online.

Complementary source: *Social Trends.*

Euromonitor plc, 60-61 Britton Street, London EC1M 5NA. Tel: 020 7251 8024. Fax: 020 7608 3149. E-mail: info@euromonitor.com. Web: www.euromonitor.com.

World of Learning

Gives details of universities, colleges, learned societies, research institutes and museums worldwide. Also available online at www.worldoflearning.com.

Companion sources: *Europa Directory of International Organizations, Europa World Yearbook.*

Europa Publications, 11 New Fetter Lane, London EC4P 4EE. Tel:

020 7822 4300. Fax: 020 7822 4329. E-mail: info.europa@tandf. co.uk. Web: www.europapublications.co.uk.

Yearbook of International Organizations

Gives contact details and activities of organizations worldwide. Also available on CD-ROM and online at www.uia.org.

Competitors: *Encyclopaedia of Associations: International Organizations, Europa Directory of International Organizations*

Comparable sources: *Directory of European Industrial & Trade Associations, Directory of European Professional & Learned Societies, Pan-European Associations, World Directory of Trade and Business Associations.*

Union of International Associations and K G Saur Verlag, Ortlerstrasse 8; D-81373 München, Germany. Tel: 00 49 089 769020. Fax: 00 49 089 76902 150. E-mail: info@saur.de. Web: www.saur.de.

Index

abstracting services: sources
    xii–xiii, 94, 95–7, 99, 101,
    102, 105, 106, 108–9
added value see answers: adding
    value
alternative answers see answers:
    compromise
American terminology 48
annuals see directories
answers ix–xi. See also enquiries,
    questions
    adding value v–vii, viii, 78–84
    characteristics 26–8
    compromise 63, 67–9, 71–2,
        76–7, 87
    editing 79–80
    e-mail 82–3
    electronic 82–3
    enhancement 81–3
    failure viii, 70–7, 87
    fax 81–2
    ideal 21–2
    imagining v–vii, viii, 26–8
    need to know 72–4
    oral 80–1
    presentation v–vii, viii, 21–2,
        80–4
    quick & dirty 68
    relevance 78–80
    sources xii–xiii, 103
    telephone 80–1
    written 81–2
articles 35–7. See also journals,
    newspapers
    sources ix–xi, xii–xiii, 92–3,
        94, 95–7, 99, 101, 102, 105,
        106, 108–9
associations see information ser-
    vices, specialist or libraries,
    special or organizations,
    specialist
audiotex 37
aural information see
    information, aural

authors: referral 74

bibliographies see sources and
    specific types e.g. articles:
    sources, books: sources
biographies see Who's Who pub-
    lications
bookmarking see web: favourites
books 30–1, 35–7
    reviews 92–3
    sources ix–xi, xii–xiii, 97, 101,
        107–8
Boolean logic 52–3
broad-based information see
    information: focus
broader terms see search terms or
    thesaurus, mini
browsing see scanning
budgets see information: cost

CD-ROMs 21, 36–9, 94. See also
    databases, portable
charged-for information services
    see information: cost or
    information brokers
charts 82–3
Chinese whispers see enquirers:
    Chinese whispers
citations see sources: citing
closed questions see questions,
    closed
complexity see information:
    complexity
comprehensive information see
    information: focus
compromise answers see answers:
    compromise
conference papers: sources 97
confidentiality see enquiries:
    confidentiality
contacts: sources ix–xi, xii–xiii,
    85, 92–3
copyright 83–4, 91
    sources 98

costs see information: cost
countries: sources 95, 100,
    106–7, 109. See also facts
    and figures: sources or sta-
    tistics: sources
customer relations 4–5, 69, 70–2,
    76–7, 81–4, 90–1

databases 35–43, 64. See also CD-
    ROMs, online services,
    teletext, web
    portable 36–43
    searching 52–3
    sources ix–xi, xii–xiii, 94,
        95–7, 98–9, 100, 101, 102,
        103, 105, 106, 108–9
dates see events and dates:
    sources
deadlines see enquiries: deadlines
diagrams see illustrations
dictionaries xii, 36–7
digital video discs 39
directories ix–xi, 35–7, 54–5, 81
    acquiring 91
    sources ix–xi, xii–xiii, 98,
        107–8
discussion lists see online
    discussion lists
disgruntled enquirers see
    enquirers, disgruntled
DIY enquiry answering see
    enquirers: helping
document supply services 92–3,
    97
do it yourself see enquirers: help-
    ing
downloading see information,
    downloaded
duration of enquiries see
    enquiries: time taken
DVDs 39
dynamic information see infor-
    mation: dynamism

e-mail see enquiries: e-mail or
    answers: e-mail
editors: referral 74
electronic media see media:
    electronic
encyclopaedias xii, 30–1, 35–7
enquirers ix–xi, 1–18
    changing the question 78–9
    Chinese whispers 2, 10–11
    competing 62–3
    disgruntled 4
    generalists 2, 12–13
    helping 23, 62–3, 67–8
    homophones 2, 10
    know-alls 3, 13–14
    malapropisms 2, 11–12
    muddlers 3, 14
    secretive 3, 4–5, 14–15
    time wasters 4–5
    types 2–3, 4–5
    unconvinced 4
enquiries v–vii, viii. See also
    answers, questions
    analysis ix–xi, 9–15
    changed 78–9
    characteristics ix–xi
    confidentiality 89
    deadlines ix–xi, 17, 61–9, 71–2,
        76–7, 88
    difficulty 63–7, 71–2, 87–8
    e-mail 1, 16, 61, 68, 73–4
    failure 20, 70–7, 87
    fax 1, 61
    learning from 85–93
    negotiation 8–17, 68, 71–2,
        76–7
    oral 1, 5, 16
    postal 1
    prioritizing 22–3, 62–3
    progress reports 69, 71
    record keeping ix–xi, 16–17,
        86–91
    referring viii, 42, 68, 71–6,
        88–90
    signing off ix–xi, 85–93
    sources xii–xiii, 103
    specialism 24
    success 86–7
    telephone 1, 5, 68
    thinking time 26, 68

    time taken 62–7, 70, 87–8
    viability ix–xi, 70–7
    written 1, 61
enquiry forms ix–xi, 16, 78–9
ethics 83 4
events and dates: sources ix–xi,
    xii–xiii, 95, 102–3, 108

facts and figures: sources ix–xi,
    xii–xv, 95, 100, 106–7, 108,
    109. See also countries:
    sources or statistics: sources
failure see answers: failure or
    enquiries: failure or sources:
    failure
FAQs see frequently asked ques-
    tions files or information
    files, internal
favourites see web: favourites
faxes see answers: fax, enquiries:
    fax
figures see facts and figures or
    statistics
focus see information: focus
forced choice questions see ques-
    tions, forced choice
frequently asked questions files
    32, 68, 90–1
funnelling questions see ques-
    tions, funnelling

generalizations see enquirers:
    generalists
graphs 82–3

handbooks see directories
help, outside see libraries, special
    or organizations, specialist
    or enquiries: referring
helping enquirers see enquirers:
    helping
historical databases see databases
    or online services or web
homonyms 47–8
homophones see enquirers:
    homophones
hypothetical questions see ques-
    tions, hypothetical
imagination see answers: imagin-
    ing

illustrations 81. See also images
images 82–3. See also illustrations
indexes 48–51
    sources ix–xi
indexing 90–1
information. See also sources
    aural 10–11
    brokers 70, 74–5
    characteristics 35–8
    complexity ix–xi, 37–8, 39–43
    cost 21, 39, 64, 68, 70–2, 74–6,
        78, 88–90
    downloaded 83–4
    dynamism ix–xi, 36–7, 39–43
    files, internal 32, 59, 90–1
    focus ix–xi, 35–6, 39–43
    overload 19–25, 79–80
    purchase
    purpose 22–3
    quality 39, 54–5, 73
    selection 21–2
    specialism 24
    rejection 19–20
information profession see
    library and information pro-
    fession
information services
    customer needs 91–2
    development xi–xi, 85–93
    promotion 91–3
    specialist 68, 71–5, 88–90, 96.
        See also libraries, special or
        organizations, specialist
    sources xii–xiii, 71–2, 96, 109
    subscribing 75–6, 89–90
information units see informa-
    tion services: specialist or
    libraries, special or organiza-
    tions, specialist
international information
    sources see sources: interna-
    tional
internet v–vii, 58–9. See also
    online services, web
    sources 101, 103, 104
interrogation techniques see
    questioning techniques
interview, reference see question-
    ing techniques
intranets 59, 90–2

journalists: referral 74
journals 36–7. *See also* articles,
  newspapers
  acquiring 92
  sources ix–xi, xii–xiii, 92–3,
    96, 107–8, 109

know-alls *see* enquirers: know-
  alls
knowledge management 90–1

leading questions *see* questions,
  leading
libraries, special 68, 71–5, 88–90,
  96. *See also* information services, specialist *or* organizations, specialist
  sources 96, 109
library and information profession v–vii
library and information services
  see information services
licensing 83–4, 91
  sources 98
logical operators *see* Boolean
  logic

magazines *see* journals *or* newspapers
malapropisms *see* enquirers:
  malapropisms
media
  characteristics ix–xi
  choice 21, 34–43, 91
  electronic v–vii, ix–xi, 35,
    38–43, 55, 64, 94
  printed v–vii, ix–xi, 35, 37–43,
    55, 64, 94
microforms 20, 34
mini-thesaurus *see* thesaurus,
  mini
misunderstandings, avoiding *see*
  questions: understanding
muddlers *see* enquirers: muddlers
multi-faceted enquiries *see* information: complexity
multiple questions *see* questions,
  multiple

narrow & specific information
  see information: focus
narrower terms *see* search terms
  or thesaurus, mini
news services, online *see* web:
  news services
newsletters, online 92
newspapers 37. *See also* articles,
  journals
  sources ix–xi, xii–xiii, 20, 96,
    108

obsessively secretive enquirers
  see enquirers, secretive
online
  discussion lists 72–4, 92
  newsletters 92
  services ix–xi, 21, 37–43, 71–2,
    75–6, 92–3, 94, 98–9, 100,
    103, 108–9. *See also* data-
    bases, internet, teletext, web
open questions *see* questions,
  open
oral enquiries and answers *see*
  answers, oral *or* enquiries,
  oral
organizations, specialist 68, 71–5,
  85, 88–90. *See also* information services, specialist *or*
  libraries, special
  sources 96, 98, 99–100, 102,
    104, 109, 110

performance data 16
periodicals *see* journals
photocopying 81–4
pictures *see* illustrations *or*
  images
portable databases *see* databases,
  portable
postal enquiries *see* enquiries,
  postal
press releases 37
print *see* media: printed
prioritizing *see* enquiries: prioritizing *or* sources: prioritizing
probing questions *see* questions,
  probing
profession, library and informa-

tion *see* library and information profession
progress reports *see* enquiries:
  progress reports
publishers: referral 74

quality of information *see* information: quality
questioning techniques viii,
  ix–xi, 1–18, 21–2
questions ix–xi, 1–18. *See also*
  enquiries, answers
  closed 6, 18
  forced choice 6–7, 18
  funnelling 8
  hypothetical 8, 18
  leading 7, 18
  misunderstandings *see* ques-
    tions: understanding
  multiple 7, 18
  open 6, 18
  probing 8–9
  supplementary viii, 5–8
  types 5–8
  understanding 2–5

rapid reading *see* reading, rapid:
  techniques
reading, rapid: techniques
  59–60. *See also* scanning
real time databases *see* databases
  or online services *or* web:
  news services
record keeping *see* enquiries:
  record keeping
reference interview *see* questioning techniques *or* questions
reference sources *see* sources *and*
  specific types e.g. directories,
  journals
references: 'see' and 'see also'
  50–1
referrals *see* enquiries: referring
related terms *see* search terms *or*
  thesaurus, mini
reliability of information *see*
  information: quality
reports, specialist 35–6
  identifying 92–3
  sources 97

root terms *see* search terms *or* thesaurus, mini

scanning 37, 92–3. *See also* reading, rapid: techniques
scheduling *see* enquiries: deadlines
'see' and 'see also' references *see* references: 'see' and 'see also'
search engines *see* web: search engines
search
  software 52–3
  strategies viii, ix–xi, 44–60
  terms viii, ix–xi, 46–51
  tools *see* web: search engines
secretive enquirers *see* enquirers, secretive
serials *see specific types* e.g. journals, directories
service development *see* information services: development
signing off *see* enquiries: signing off
single-issue enquiries *see* information: complexity
software: licensing
sources v–vii, ix–xi, xii–xiii, 20, 94–110. *See also* information
  acquiring 85, 90–1, 92–3
  appropriateness 44–6, 71–2
  basic xii–xiii, 30–2, 63, 103, 107–8
  citing 80–3
  eliminating 24–5
  evaluating 31, 90–91
  exploiting 92–3
  failure 64, 70–7
  identifying ix–xi, xii–xiii, 24–5, 26–32, 90–1
  international ix–xi, xii–xiii, 31, 95, 99–100, 101, 104, 106, 107, 108, 109, 110
  prioritizing 22, 44–6, 79–80
  promoting 91
  recording ix–xi, 90–1

relevance 44–6, 71–2
selecting 79–80
specialism 24
suggesting 67, 76–7
timeliness 44–6, 71–2
types 24–5, 28–30
unpublished v–vii, 90–1
specialism *see* enquiries: specialism, sources: specialism
specialist organizations *see* organizations, specialist
specific information *see* information: focus
speed of enquiries *see* enquiries: time taken
spellings, variant 47
spreadsheets 82–3
static information *see* information: dynamism
statistics ix–xi, xii–xiii, 35–7, 81–3
  sources ix–xi, xii–xiii, 94–5, 100, 104–5, 106, 107–8, 109. *See also* countries: sources *or* facts and figures: sources
subject indexes *see* indexes
subscribing to information services *see* information services: subscribing
supplementary questions *see* questions, supplementary
synonymous terms *see* search terms *or* thesaurus, mini

telephone *see* answers: telephone *or* audiotex *or* enquiries: telephone
teletext 37. *See also* databases, online services, web
terminology *see* search terms
textbooks s*ee* books
thesaurus, mini viii, ix–xi, 48–51
time management 61–9
time taken *see* enquiries: time taken
time-wasters *see* enquirers: time-wasters

timetabling *see* enquiries: deadlines

unconvinced enquirers *see* enquirers, unconvinced
urgency *see* enquiries: deadlines
URLs *see* web: addresses

value, adding *see* answers: adding value
verbal enquiries and answers *see* answers, oral *or* enquiries, oral
viability *see* enquiries: viability
videotex *see* teletext
vital tasks *see* enquiries: deadlines

web v–vii 37–8, 53–9, 94. *See also* databases, internet, online discussion lists, online services, teletext
  addresses 57–8
  appropriateness 55
  country codes 58
  domains 57–8
  favourites 32, 59, 89
  news services ix–xi, xii–xiii, 21, 37
  sources 96
  search engines v–vii, 55–7, 58–9
  search techniques 53–9
  sites ix–xi, xii–xiii, 53–9
  sources ix–xi, xii–xiii, 54–5, 58–9, 73–4, 101, 103, 104
Who? What? When? Where? Why? How? ix–xi, 9–15, 18. *See also* enquiries: analysis
Who's Who publications xii
word processing 82–3
world wide web *see* web

yearbooks *see* directories